Understanding
Multivariate Research

Understanding Multivariate Research

A Primer for Beginning Social Scientists

William D. Berry
Florida State University

Mitchell S. Sanders
Florida State University

Westview Press
A Member of the Perseus Books Group

Copyright © 2000 by Westview Press, A Member of the Perseus Books Group

Published in 2000 in the United States of America by Westview Press, 5500 Central Avenue, Boulder, Colorado 80301-2877, and in the United Kingdom by Westview Press, 12 Hid's Copse Road, Cumnor Hill, Oxford OX2 9JJ

Find us on the World Wide Web at www.westviewpress.com

Library of Congress Cataloging-in-Publication Data
Berry, William Dale.
    Understanding multivariate research : a primer for beginning social scientists / William D. Berry, Mitchell S. Sanders.
        p.   cm.
    Includes bibliographical references and index.
    ISBN 0-8133-9971-8 (pbk.)
    1. Social sciences—Research—Methodology.   2. Multivariate analysis.
3. Regression analysis.   I. Sanders, Mitchell S.   II. Title.   III. Series.

H62 .B454   2000
300'.7'2—dc21
                                                                99-057762

The paper used in this publication meets the requirements of the American National Standard for Permanence of Paper for Printed Library Materials Z39.48-1984.

10   9   8   7   6   5   4   3   2   1

Contents

Tables and Figures

Preface for
Teachers and Students

If social science departments wanted to structure their graduate programs to allow students to make the best use of their training in research methodology, they would probably devote their students' first semester of course work to methods training, using applications from the literature as illustrations but delaying substantive courses until students had completed a department's core methods courses. Of course, very few programs are structured in this fashion. Indeed, such a course schedule would likely leave students frustrated with having to delay beginning the study of human affairs until the second semester.

In most graduate programs the core methods sequence is stretched over two or three semesters. A typical three-semester version includes philosophy of science and research design in the first semester, introductory statistics in the second, and multivariate analysis—emphasizing regression—in the third. So in practice, exposure to regression analysis and other multivariate techniques often does not come until well into a student's second or third semester in graduate school. However, before this exposure, students are taking substantive courses and reading literature that relies on regression and other, similar techniques. In effect, we have been teaching students to evaluate quantitative social science research much like parents who teach their young children to swim by throwing them into the middle of a pool without any prior instruction. Our students may learn to "swim"—to survive—but they certainly won't have any fun doing so.

As teachers, we ought to do better. Yet virtually all textbooks covering multivariate methods—even those intended for introductory courses—present the techniques assuming students (1) have learned the basic principles of probability theory and statistical inference (so that they can make sense of standard errors, t-tests for coefficient estimates, and confidence intervals), and (2) are familiar with the concept of a distribution and the use of univariate descriptive statistics for measuring central tendency and dispersion of distributions.

It is entirely reasonable that presentations of techniques such as regression analysis assume such a background in statistics, since if one is going to learn both introductory inferential statistics and regression, it *is* more efficient to start with statistics. But students can learn a great deal about regression and other multivariate methods with virtually no background in statistics; they can acquire a conceptual understanding of some of the key assumptions of these techniques and an ability to interpret the meaning of the coefficients estimated. Thus, we can give students an entry-level background in multivariate analysis very early in their graduate training, thereby allowing them to understand the essential elements of research that relies on such analysis before they undertake more thorough training in multivariate analysis later in their careers.

This book offers a conceptual introduction to regression analysis and related techniques that can be assigned to graduate students at the beginning of their first semester, or even the summer before starting school. We assume that students come to the book with a "clean slate"—that they have no knowledge of descriptive or inferential statistics or of social science research design. We present all topics without relying on the mathematical language of probability theory and statistical inference. In fact, the math is limited to some simple algebra, which we review early on. Furthermore, we believe that the material presented can be learned by a conscientious student, through multiple readings, with little or no time devoted to attending accompanying class lectures. The book is short, so that even three or four close readings do not require an excessive investment of time.

The text is divided into two major parts. The first covers basic topics in regression analysis and is restricted to linear additive models. The second extends the regression model in several ways:

to nonlinear and nonadditive models, to "causal models" containing more than a single equation, and to probit and logit models with dichotomous dependent variables. Unless students are going to have frequent exposure to research articles relying on these advanced techniques, the second part of the book can be treated as reference material—to be read a couple of times, and then reviewed in greater detail when faced with a study relying on one of these techniques.

The book is also appropriate for some undergraduate students. Since it has no statistics prerequisite, its appropriateness for undergraduates is determined by whether they will be expected to read original research relying on multivariate analysis. If the students are deemed capable of reading articles reporting on quantitative research, clearly they should be able to understand this introduction to quantitative methods. We can envision this book being assigned as a text in an undergraduate methods course in a department in which students in junior- and senior-level courses are asked to read quantitative research. However, we can also see it being assigned by instructors in departments without an undergraduate research methods requirement, as preliminary reading in a course in which students will be reading original quantitative research. If the articles to be read rely only on linear, additive regression models, students might be assigned just the first part of this book, through Chapter 5.

It would be terrific if we could publish a different version of this book for each social science discipline, so that each student could see examples drawn exclusively from the discipline he or she has chosen to study. Since this is not feasible, we wrote a single version that relies on illustrations drawn from research across a variety of disciplines. To make them accessible to students with varied backgrounds, we chose examples that we believe could be understood without any background in the parent discipline. Indeed, for one recurring illustration, we turn away from the social sciences to consider the factors determining a person's weight, since this is a topic about which all readers should have a certain amount of intuition.

We close this preface with some encouragement and advice for students. Assuming the material in this book is new to you, do not expect to understand—or remember—all of it after just one reading. There is much to learn and synthesize. However, with each additional reading, more and more aspects of the material should become clear. Thus, we hope you have the patience to undertake several readings even if your principal reaction to your first exposure is frustration. We are confident that your persistence will be rewarded!

At various points in the text, we include brief exercises that you may use to test your knowledge of the topics discussed. These exercises are enclosed in brackets (i.e., [. . .]) and prefaced, for easy identification, with a pair of exclamation points (!!). The text immediately following an exercise gives the correct answer. However, the design of the text allows these bracketed exercises to be ignored without any loss of continuity of our presentation. Indeed, we suggest skipping the exercises when reading the book for the first time, but pausing to work through them on additional readings. If you can complete these exercises successfully, this is a strong indication that you are absorbing the material presented.

William D. Berry
Mitchell S. Sanders

Acknowledgments

This book began as a paper written for graduate students in political science at Florida State University in 1994. Since then it has gone through numerous revisions before assuming its current form. We wish to thank the colleagues who provided helpful comments on various previous versions (even though several of these folks read the book so long ago that they will probably will not remember having done so!): Charles Barrilleaux, Daniel Berry, Frances Berry, Belinda Davis, Aubrey Jewett, Gary King, Tatiana Kostadinova, Doug Lemke, Andrew Long, Andrew Martin, Glenn Mitchell, Evan Ringquist, and Kevin Wang. The students in two Florida State graduate courses on research methods also reviewed drafts of the book: Berry's spring 1994 seminar, and Will Moore's fall 1999 seminar. We are very grateful to both classes. Because our writing stretched over such a long period, and the years have taken a toll on our memories, we have undoubtedly failed to thank some who reviewed early drafts. We apologize to any who have been inadvertently omitted.

W. D. B.
M. S. S.

Understanding
Multivariate Research

1

Introduction

The Concept of Causation

Much social science research is designed to test hypotheses (or propositions) about *causation*. Such hypotheses take the form of an assertion that if *something* (e.g., some event) occurs, then *something else* will happen as a result. Among nations, we might assert that population growth causes (or influences) economic growth. Among individuals, we might believe that body weight is influenced by food consumption. In a causal hypothesis, the phenomenon that is explained is called the *dependent variable*. It is called a *variable* because we are conceiving of something that can "vary" across a set of cases (e.g., persons or nations); it is called *dependent* because of the assertion of causation: its value is hypothesized to be dependent on the value of some other variable. In our examples the dependent variables are a nation's economic growth and an individual's weight. The other variable in the hypothesis—the one that is expected to influence the dependent variable—is called the *independent* (or *explanatory*) *variable*. Population growth is thought to be an independent variable affecting a nation's economic growth; a person's food consumption is conceived as an independent variable influencing his or her weight. There are numerous synonyms for the terms independent and dependent variable in the social sciences. Table 1.1 lists the most common terms.

Let us take a closer look at what it means to claim that one variable influences another. The most common conception of causa-

TABLE 1.1   Synonyms for Independent and Dependent Variable

Independent Variable	*Dependent Variable*
Explanatory variable	Explained variable
Exogenous variable	Endogenous variable
Predictor variable	Response variable
	Target variable

SOURCE: Modified from Maddala (1992, 61).

tion focuses on the *responsiveness* of one variable to a change in the value of the other. When we claim that food intake influences body weight, we are implicitly arguing that if we were able to increase a person's food consumption while holding everything else constant, the individual's weight will change. The clause "while holding everything else constant" is important, because if other variables change at the same time as food consumption, the individual's weight change could be a response to a change in one or more other factors rather than the increase in food consumption.

More generally, when we claim that some variable, X, influences another variable, Y, we mean that if all other variables could be held constant, then a change in the value of X would result in a change in the value of Y. We can also develop a measure of the *magnitude* (or strength) of the impact of X on Y by focusing on the size of the change in the value of Y occurring in response to some fixed increase in X. If a given increase in X leads to a 10-unit decrease in Y in one environment, but to a 5-unit decrease in another context, the former impact can be deemed twice as strong as the latter. (Several expressions are used interchangeably by social scientists to convey an assertion of causation; "X causes Y," "X influences Y," "X affects Y," and "X has an impact on Y" are synonymous. The custom of using the symbol Y to denote a dependent variable and X to indicate an independent variable is deeply ingrained in the social science literature, and we shall follow this custom throughout the book.)

Experimental Research

Suppose we wish to test the hypothesis that an independent variable X influences a dependent variable Y using empirical analysis.

(*Empirical* analysis refers to analysis based on *observation.*) The ideal way to do so would be to conduct an *experiment.* Your familiarity with experiments probably dates back to your first science class in elementary school. However, it is important to refresh our memories on the specific features of an experiment. To illustrate, say we design an experiment to test the claim that a fictitious new drug—a pill called Mirapill—helps to prevent children from getting the fictitious disease turkey pox. The *population* in question—that is, the cases to which the hypothesis is meant to apply—is children who have not had turkey pox. The independent variable is whether or not a child is given Mirapill, and the dependent variable is the probability that the child will get the disease.

In an experiment designed to test whether Mirapill reduces the probability of getting turkey pox, we would begin by taking a random sample—perhaps 1,000 subjects—from the population of children who have never had turkey pox. (For the sample to be *random,* every member of the population must have the same chance of being included in the sample.) These 1,000 children then would be randomly assigned to two groups. One group of 500 would be called the *experimental group,* and the other, the *control group.*

Randomness—both in the selection of subjects from the population and in the assignment of subjects to the experimental and control groups—is critical to the validity of an experiment. Statisticians have discovered that if a sample is selected randomly and is large enough (1,000 is certainly sufficient), it is likely to be *representative,* in every respect, of the larger population from which it is drawn.[1] This means that we can learn almost as much by observing the sample as by observing the full population, yet the former is generally far less expensive and time consuming. In an ex-

---

[1] A large sample is necessary for this claim to hold, because the smaller a sample, the more likely it is to be unrepresentative of the population. To get a sense of why this is true, imagine flipping a fair coin four times. Although getting half heads and half tails is the most likely outcome, you probably would not be amazed to get three heads and one tails (i.e., three-quarters heads). But if you were to flip the coin 100 times, you likely would be quite surprised if you got three-fourths heads (i.e., a 75–25 outcome). This is because a small sample of coin flips is more likely to be unrepresentative of the population (in which heads and tails occur equally often) than a large sample.

periment, we observe the random sample and, on the basis of what we learn, draw an *inference* about whether the hypothesis is likely to be true in the overall population. Similarly, random *assignment* of the children in the sample to the two groups makes it very likely that the groups will be nearly equivalent *in every way*. For example, the two groups of children should be almost equally likely to be genetically predisposed to get turkey pox. The two groups also should be nearly equally likely to be exposed to turkey pox through contact with other children.

In the next step of the experiment, the children in the experimental group would be given Mirapill, whereas those in the control group would receive a *placebo*. (A good placebo would be a pill that looks exactly like Mirapill but contains no medicine.) After the pills are administered, both groups would be observed for a period, and we would determine how many children in each group contracted turkey pox. If fewer children in the experimental group than in the control group got the illness, this would be evidence supporting the hypothesis that Mirapill helps to prevent turkey pox. Furthermore, the difference between the two groups in the number of children contracting the disease would serve as a measure of the strength of Mirapill's impact as a preventive. If many fewer children in the experimental group got sick, this would suggest that Mirapill has a strong effect. If only slightly fewer experimental group children came down with turkey pox, this would mean that the effect is probably weak.

Suppose we conduct this experiment and find that the incidence of turkey pox is substantially lower in the experimental group. Why would this be convincing evidence that Mirapill prevents turkey pox? To see why, recall what we mean when we say that X causes Y: if all other variables were held constant, then a change in the value of X would lead to a change in the value of Y. Our experiment gives us just the information we need to assess a claim of causation. We find out what happens to the dependent variable (the probability of getting turkey pox) when we change the value of the independent variable (receiving or not receiving Mirapill) when all other variables are held constant. (Saying that the experimental and control groups are nearly equivalent in every way—as a consequence of random assignment of children to the two groups—is the same as saying that all variables are held nearly constant from one group to the other.) In other words, random assignment of children to the control and experimental groups eliminates all explanations other than Mirapill for the difference in disease incidence between the two groups. For instance, a difference between the two groups in genetic susceptibility to turkey pox is unlikely to be responsible for the difference in disease incidence, because randomness of assignment makes it likely that varying degrees of genetic susceptibility are distributed evenly between the two groups, and thus likely that the two groups are similarly predisposed to getting turkey pox. Also, the fact that both groups were given some pill—either Mirapill or a placebo—allows us to reject the mere taking of some pill as a possible cause of the lower incidence of turkey pox in the experimental group.

The Logic Underlying Regression Analysis

Consider the hypothesis that food intake influences body weight. In principle, we could test this hypothesis experimentally, by randomly selecting subjects from the population of adults and then randomly assigning different levels of food intake to these subjects. But in practice, such a strategy would not be feasible, since it would require those being studied to tolerate an enormous degree of intrusion into their daily lives by permitting us to control how much they eat. An alternative (and more realistic) plan would be to allow the subjects to eat what they want, but to measure their food consumption and, in one way or another, compare the body weights of "small eaters" to those of "big eaters." If we find that those who eat a lot tend to be heavier than those who consume less, we would claim support for the hypothesis.

For many social science hypotheses, it is also infeasible to manipulate the independent variable experimentally. For example, if we were studying lobbying (i.e., attempts by individuals and groups to influence government officials) and we wanted to test the hypothesis that members of Congress in leadership positions are lobbied more heavily than members who are not in leadership positions, we would not be able to intervene and impose our own leadership choices on Congress. Instead, we can observe Congress as it exists and determine whether there are different patterns of lobbying activity for leaders than for nonleaders. Similarly, to test the hypothesis that population growth affects economic development, it obviously would be impossible to run an experiment in which we randomly assign different levels of population growth to nations. However, we can observe the nations of the world and determine whether those countries whose populations are growing fastest are also those whose economies are expanding most quickly. *Regression analysis* is a *non*experimental technique for extracting this sort of information from a sample of data. In this chapter and the next, we examine the simplest form of regression, *bivariate* (or two-variable) regression, which involves a single independent variable hypothesized to influence a dependent variable. In subsequent chapters we consider *multivariate* (or *multiple*) regression, which involves two or more independent variables presumed to influence the same dependent variable.

Although regression analysis often is more feasible than experimental research, it cannot provide as convincing evidence of causation as an experiment. As we have seen, in an experiment, random assignment of the value of the independent variable to subjects enables the researcher to assess the response of the dependent variable to a change in the independent variable *when all other variables that influence the dependent variable are held constant.* In nonexperimental research relying on regression, we forgo random assignment of the value of the independent variable and instead accept the values that the cases being analyzed happen to have. The result is that when we use regression, we estimate the change in the dependent variable associated with a given change in an independent variable *when the other independent variables in the regression analysis are held constant.* This falls well short of the experimental design's ability to hold constant *all* variables that influence the dependent variable.

Consequently, researchers should use regression analysis to test a hypothesis that X influences Y only when they have a *theory* that explains *why* it makes sense to expect this causal relationship. Note that in experimental research, such a theory is not essential. For example, sometimes scientists confirm that a new drug is effective using experimental research, even when they do not know *why* the drug works. But conducting nonexperimental research without a theory can lead to highly deceptive conclusions. For instance, if we were to examine fires, we would probably find that fire damage was most severe when a large number of fire trucks were on the scene—since both fire damage and number of fire trucks should rise with the size of the fire (Weisberg, Krosnick, and Bowen 1989). If so, bivariate regression analysis with fire damage as the dependent variable and the number of fire trucks present as the independent variable would generate apparent support for the (preposterous) hypothesis that fire trucks cause fire damage. What should prevent us from arriving at this erroneous conclusion is the absence of a plausible theory to suggest why fire trucks should cause damage—indeed, without such a theory, we should be unwilling to conduct regression analysis to test this hypothesis in the first place.

Some Necessary Math Background

Representing Data in a Graph

Suppose we have measured the values (or scores) of a set of cases (e.g., persons, organizations, or nations) on two variables, **X** and **Y**. Returning to one of our earlier examples, let us say that we observe the food intake and the body weight of four people. We measure weight in pounds and denote this variable by the label **WEIGHT**. Our measure of food intake is average daily food consumption in calories during the year prior to the observation of weight, and we denote this variable by the label **FOOD**.[2] Our observations are presented in Table 1.2.

We can portray these data in a graph by designating food intake as the horizontal axis (or what mathematicians call the x-axis) and body weight as the vertical axis (the y-axis) and plotting four points on the graph, one for each person. (The nearly uniform custom in the social sciences is to use the horizontal axis for the independent variable and the vertical axis for the dependent variable.) The position of each point is determined by the values of **FOOD** and **WEIGHT** for the associated person. For example, in

---

[2]This example is a modified version of an illustration presented in Berry 1993.

TABLE 1.2   Observations for Food Intake and Body Weight

	X = FOOD	Y = WEIGHT
Bob	3,000	190
Carol	1,100	120
Ted	2,300	155
Alice	1,400	140

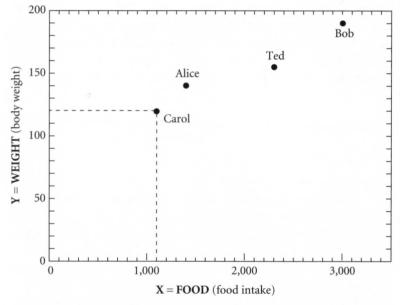

FIGURE 1.1   Data on food intake and body weight for four individuals

the graph in Figure 1.1, the lower left point representing Carol is positioned 1,100 units out on the horizontal axis (denoting **FOOD**) and 120 units up on the vertical axis (denoting **WEIGHT**).

This type of graph is called a *scatterplot* (or sometimes *scatter diagram* or *scattergram*), because it *plots* the *scattered* X and Y values. The great advantage of the graphical presentation of these data over the tabular format is that the graph allows us more easily to observe the *relationship* between food intake and body weight.

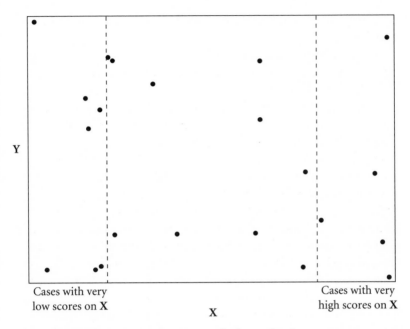

Cases with very
low scores on **X**

Cases with very
high scores on **X**

X

FIGURE 1.2   Two variables that are completely unrelated

This is particularly true when there are a large number of cases, which makes it difficult or impossible to observe patterns within data presented in columns. For the four individuals whose food intake and body weight are plotted in Figure 1.1, it appears that high values on **WEIGHT** tend to be associated with high values on **FOOD**. In contrast, the graph in Figure 1.2 shows a situation in which there is no relationship between two variables for a group of twenty cases. We say that two variables, **X** and **Y**, are *completely unrelated* (or that there is *no relationship* between them) if knowledge of the value of **X** for a case would provide no help at all in predicting the value of **Y** for that case. For the data plotted in Figure 1.2, if we are told that a case has a very high score on **X**, it is of no help to us in predicting the case's score on **Y**, since cases having high values on **X** have scores on **Y** spread all the way from very low to very high. The same is true for cases having a low value on **X**. In contrast, for the data in Figure 1.1, knowledge that a case has a high value on **X** would make a prediction that the case also has a high score on Y much more reasonable than a prediction of a low score on Y.

Social scientists use the term *correlation* as one way to describe the strength of the relationship between two variables. You may have heard this term used in everyday discourse to express the closeness of a relationship. The formal measure of correlation is called the *correlation coefficient,* and it is nearly always denoted by a lowercase *r*. The correlation coefficient ranges from −1 to +1. A correlation coefficient of zero means that there is no relationship between X and Y; the relationship in Figure 1.2, for example, is one for which *r* = 0. As *r* increases or decreases from zero, the relationship becomes stronger. A *positive* correlation coefficient—a coefficient greater than zero—implies a relationship in which, as the value of X increases over cases, the value of Y tends to increase too (as in Figure 1.1). In contrast, a *negative* correlation coefficient—less than zero—means that the value of Y tends to decrease as the value of X increases. The extreme values for *r* of +1 and −1 indicate a *perfect linear relationship,* that is, one in which all points in the scatterplot fall exactly on a line.

Although the correlation coefficient provides useful information about how well we can predict values of Y if we know X, it does not tell us anything about *how responsive* Y is to a change in X—that is, *how much* Y changes for a given change in X. Therefore, the correlation coefficient does not help us to assess the *strength* of X's impact on Y. For example, consider the two scatterplots in Figure 1.3. The relationships depicted are equal in strength in terms of the correlation coefficient; in both *r* = +0.75. Yet, in a different sense, we would consider the relationship shown in scatterplot A to be stronger than that shown in scatterplot B. Note how the scattering of dots rises more rapidly from left to right in A than in B. Thus, as the value of X increases, the value of Y increases by a larger amount in scatterplot A than in scatterplot B. This makes it clear that Y is more *responsive* to a change in X in A than in B. Regression analysis measures the strength of the relationship between X and Y in this sense of responsiveness. For this reason, regression analysis is more useful for studying causation than is calculating a correlation coefficient.

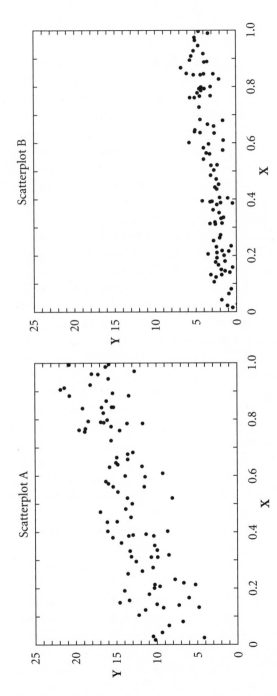

FIGURE 1.3   Two scatterplots with correlation coefficients of +0.75

Lines and Their Equations

Scatterplots—such as those graphed in Figures 1.1, 1.2, and 1.3—show the values of specific cases on the variables X and Y. We can also graph *lines* expressing the relationship between X and Y, such as the lines in Figure 1.4. Social scientists use the term *intercept* to denote the value of Y when X equals zero, or equivalently, the point at which the line intersects the vertical axis. (Mathematicians would call the intercept the y-intercept. But social scientists refer to it simply as the intercept, since they seldom have any reason to calculate the x-intercept.) [!! *Try to determine the intercept of each line in Figure 1.4.*] Thus, the intercept of the dotted line in Figure 1.4 is 1, and that of the solid line is 3.

The *slope* of a line is defined as the change in Y associated with a one-unit increase in X. Because a line is straight, the slope of a line is the same regardless of the level of X at which it is calculated. [!! *Determine the slope of each line in Figure 1.4.*] In the case of the dotted line in Figure 1.4, an increase of one unit in X is associated with an increase of two units in Y, so the slope is 2. In contrast, for the solid line, a one-unit increase in X yields a decrease of one-quarter unit in Y (i.e., a change of minus one-fourth in Y), so the slope of the line is –0.25. (Another way to say this is that an increase of four units in X is associated with a decrease of one unit in Y.) Paralleling the distinction between positive and negative correlations, lines that slope upward from left to right (like the dotted line in Figure 1.4), and thus have a positive slope, are described as reflecting positive relationships, whereas lines that slope downward (like the solid line in Figure 1.4) are said to indicate negative relationships.

The mathematical equation for a line takes a simple form:

$$Y_i = b_0 + b_1 X_i.$$

This equation may be familiar to you from high school algebra courses, where you probably learned that the equation for a line takes the form

$$Y = mX + b,$$

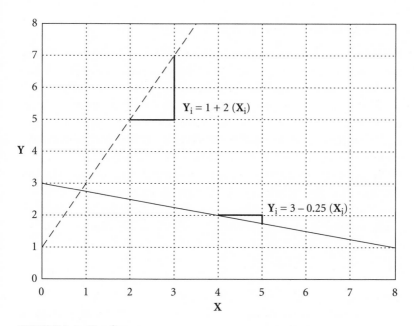

FIGURE 1.4 Two lines

where m denotes the slope and b is the y-intercept. However, social scientists usually use some symbol involving "b" (or the Greek equivalent, β) to denote the slope, and use subscripts to distinguish the slope from the intercept.

We include the subscript *i* on the variables X and Y to denote the case being observed. Thus X_i—pronounced "X-sub-i"—denotes the value of the variable X for case *i*. Since the intercept of the dotted line in Figure 1.4 is 1 and its slope is 2, its equation can be written

$$Y_i = 1 + 2X_i,$$

or sometimes, more simply (without the case subscripts), as

$$Y = 1 + 2X.$$

The equation for the solid line is expressed as

$$Y_i = 3 - 0.25X_i \ [\text{or } Y = 3 - 0.25X].$$

The Slope as the Magnitude of the Impact of X on Y

If we have a plausible theory explaining how X influences Y, and we have a graph of a line showing the relationship between X and Y when all other variables influencing Y are held constant, then the slope of the line tells us the magnitude of the impact of X on Y, since it shows us how much Y changes in response to a change in X. *It is for this reason that the slope is considered the fundamental measure of the size of the impact of one variable on another.*

To return to our earlier example, assume that food intake has an effect on body weight, and that the relationship between food intake and the weight of an individual (when all other influences on weight are held constant at specific values) is described by the line

$$\textbf{WEIGHT}_i = 75 + 0.036(\textbf{FOOD}_i).$$

Recalling that **WEIGHT** is measured in pounds and **FOOD** in calories, the equation implies that the impact of food intake on body weight can be described as one in which a 1 calorie increase in average daily food intake results in an increase of 0.036 pounds in an individual's weight. Equivalently, an increase of 100 calories boosts expected weight 3.6 (= 100 × 0.036) pounds.[3]

---

[3]In the social sciences, the asterisk (*) or dot (·) sometimes is used to indicate multiplication instead of "×".

2

The Bivariate Regression Model

The Equation

Suppose we believe that X is a cause of Y in some population. The *bivariate regression equation* expresses the value of Y for any case *i* in terms of the intercept (b_0), the value of X for case *i*, the slope coefficient (b_1), and the value of an *error term* (or *disturbance term*), e, for case *i*:

$$(2.1) \qquad Y_i = b_0 + b_1 X_i + e_i.$$

Note that X, Y, and e have a case subscript, i, whereas the intercept (b0) and the slope coefficient (b1) do not. This is because X, Y, and e are variables, the value of which will vary from case to case, but the intercept and slope are constant.

The first part of equation 2.1 ($Y_i = b_0 + b_1 X_i$) you will recognize as the equation for a line; this line is known as the *regression line*. The last term, the error term e, is included because in the real world, even if X has a very strong effect on Y, we would not expect cases to have values for X and Y that fall *exactly* on the regression line. Instead, other factors likely affect Y so that the Y value for a particular case is likely to fall above or below the line. These other factors are encompassed in the error term, **e**. Another way to think of this is that for any case *i*, the regression line $Y_i = b_0 + b_1X_i$ associates the most likely value (also called the *expected value*) for the dependent variable **Y** with the **X** value for that case. Then the error term e_i represents the deviation of the actual value of the dependent variable for the case from this most likely value.

Again, consider the relationship between food intake and body weight. While food intake definitely influences a person's weight, it does not determine weight exactly. There are other variables that affect weight; these include height, sex, age, and amount of exercise. The combined effect of these variables and all other factors determining weight is represented by the error term, **e**. Consequently, we would express the relationship between an individual's food intake and his or her weight as follows:

(2.2) $\text{WEIGHT}_i = b_0 + b_1(\text{FOOD}_i) + e_i.$

The goal of empirical research about the impact of food consumption on weight using regression analysis would be to measure the intercept (b_0) and the slope coefficient (b_1) of equation 2.2. But just as an illustration, suppose we know these values—that in a population, $b_0 = 75$ and $b_1 = 0.036$ (as in the earlier example). Equation 2.2 can thus be written

(2.3) $\text{WEIGHT}_i = 75 + 0.036(\text{FOOD}_i) + e_i.$

Figure 2.1 depicts the relationship expressed in equation 2.3 in a graph. The line represents the equation

(2.4) $\text{WEIGHT}_i = 75 + 0.036(\text{FOOD}_i)$

and shows the expected (or most likely) weight for each value of food intake. The points represent the values of **FOOD** and **WEIGHT** for a sample of 22 cases from the larger population. Note that the points do not fall exactly on this line because of the contribution of the disturbance term e_i for each case. In Figure 2.1 we can observe the three important elements of a regression equation: the intercept, the slope coefficient, and the error term.

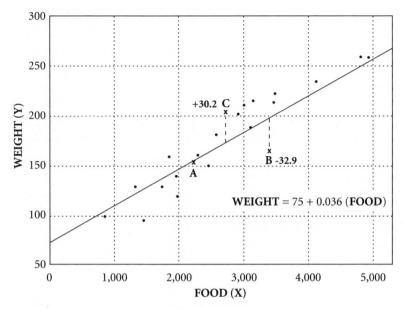

FIGURE 2.1   Graphical representation of bivariate regression equation 2.4
NOTE: Three points on the graph, labeled A, B, and C, are denoted by an "x" rather than a dot.

The Intercept

The intercept, b_0, of a regression equation can be interpreted as the expected value of Y for cases having a score of zero on X. In a graph, it is the value at which the regression line intersects the vertical axis. In some applications of regression, an intercept conveys useful substantive information. For example, imagine a study of candidates for Congress. In a regression with the percentage of the vote received as the dependent variable and campaign expenditure as the independent variable, the intercept is the expected percentage of the vote for a candidate with zero campaign spending. Thus, it tells us how a candidate who spends no money could be expected to fare on election day.

In other situations, the intercept is less meaningful, and in some cases it even yields a nonsensical interpretation. [!! *Interpret the meaning of the intercept in Figure 2.1.*] In the graph in Figure 2.1 the intercept is 75, implying that the expected weight of an individual with a food intake of zero calories (i.e., a person who never eats) is 75 pounds. Of course, this interpretation is ridiculous, since someone who never ate would die. But this does not mean that the regression model is wrong; rather, by interpreting the intercept as we have, we have made the mistake of applying the regression model to determine the expected weight of an individual outside the range of plausible values for food intake. Indeed, if in the population of individuals under consideration, average daily food intake ranges from 800 calories to 5,000 calories, the intercept would have *no* substantive meaning. However, note that the intercept is nothing more than an expected value of the dependent variable at one particular value of the independent variable, zero, and the regression equation can be used to determine the expected weight of individuals with other levels of food consumption. For instance, a person eating an extremely low amount—say, 800 calories per day—has an expected weight of $75 + (0.036 \times 800) = 75 + 28.8 = 103.8$ pounds.

The Slope Coefficient

Whereas the intercept may or may not have substantive meaning in a given application of regression, the slope coefficient is always relevant. The slope coefficient, b_1, for a regression model (sometimes called the *regression coefficient* or the *regression parameter,* or simply the *slope*) can be viewed as a measure of the effect of X on Y; it tells us the change in the expected (or average) value of Y resulting from a one-unit increase in X. [!! *Interpret the meaning of the slope coefficient, 0.036, in Figure 2.1.*] In Figure 2.1, since food intake is measured in calories and weight is measured in pounds, the slope of 0.036 indicates that an increase of 1 calorie in average daily intake results in an increase in expected weight of 0.036 pounds (i.e., about one-half ounce). However, since 1 calorie represents such a small amount of food, it would be more useful to describe the response of body weight to a more substantial change in consumption. For example, we could state that if an individual increased her daily intake by 500 calories, we would expect her weight to increase by 18 (i.e., 500×0.036) pounds.

The Error or Disturbance Term

The error or disturbance term, e, represents the combined effect of all other variables (excluding X) that have an impact on the dependent variable, plus any "inherent randomness" in the determination of the value of the dependent variable. (The rationale for the "randomness" component is that the behavior of the units typically studied by social scientists—be they individuals, organizations, U.S. states, nations, or other units—is sufficiently complex that we could never completely account for that behavior with one independent variable, or even with a large set of independent variables; some part of the behavior is essentially random and thus inexplicable.) This interpretation of the error term implies the following. For a given case, when the combined impact of all the variables influencing Y (besides X) and "randomness" makes the value of Y for the case *greater* than the expected value of Y for a case with that value of X, then the error term for the case is *positive*. If instead the combined impact of these factors makes the value of Y for the case *less* than the expected value of Y for the case, then the value of the error term is *negative*.

In our weight regression equation (2.3), the error term reflects the combined impact of all variables that influence a person's weight in addition to food intake, plus any inherent randomness in the process by which an individual's weight is determined. We have already speculated that the variables reflected in the disturbance term include height, sex, age, and amount of exercise, and undoubtedly other variables could be added to the list. In Figure 2.1, consider the case denoted by A, with a **FOOD** value of 2,232. Using equation 2.4, we can calculate that the expected value of **WEIGHT** for the case is $75 + 0.036(\textbf{FOOD}_i) = 75 + (0.036 \times 2{,}232) = 155.4$. The error term for this case is very small at -1.2, and so the point for A is just below the regression line. Thus, equation 2.3 tells us that the actual Y value for this case is 154.2 (the expected value of Y, 155.4, minus 1.2). Turn your attention now to point B, with a **FOOD** value of 3,400. The error term for this case, by contrast, is large and negative at -32.9, so the **WEIGHT** value for the case (164.5) falls well below its expected level of $75 + (0.036 \times$

3,400) = 197.4, and thus the point for B is substantially below the regression line. C, finally, denotes a case for which the disturbance term is large and positive at +30.2.

Some Necessary Assumptions

In constructing Figure 2.1, we assumed that we knew the intercept and the slope coefficient for the regression line characterizing the effect of food intake on weight in the population of interest. Of course, in the real world of research, we do not know the true values of these coefficients in the population. Typically we have data for a sample of cases randomly selected from the population[1] and we have to estimate the coefficients of the equation from the sample data. It is important to understand that several assumptions must be met for the data to yield good estimates of the population coefficients and that if any of these assumptions are violated, we cannot be confident that estimates of the intercept and the slope are reasonable estimates of the true values of the coefficients in the population. Some of these assumptions are beyond the scope of this book, since understanding their precise meaning requires a knowledge of statistics, but some of the critical assumptions can be understood readily without any background in statistics.

Assumption 1: The independent variable either is measured at the interval level, or is dichotomous.   A *dichotomous* variable (sometimes called a *binary* variable, or a *dummy* variable) is one that can take on only two possible values. One example is an individual's sex, which of course can be only male or female. A variable measured at the *interval level* is one for which any one-unit difference in numerical scores (e.g., that between 2 and 3, or between 456 and 457) reflects the same difference in the amount of the property being measured. Interval-level variables can be restricted to a small number of values (as few as three) or can take on many different values. A family's annual income in dollars is an interval-level variable, since a difference of one unit (i.e., one dollar) re-

---

[1]Recall that a randomly selected sample is one in which every member of the population has an equal chance of being included.

flects a constant difference in the property being measured—income. (The income difference between $35,000 and $35,001 is the same as the income difference between $45,000 and $45,001.) The number of children in a family is also measured at the interval level, though it is constrained to a much smaller number of values than is income. Often, interval-level variables take the form of a "count"—as in income measured in *dollars,* population measured in *persons,* or age measured in *years*—or the ratio of two counts (as in the per capita income of a nation, measured by total income in dollars divided by total persons).

Some variables are neither dichotomous nor interval-level variables and therefore should not be used as the independent variable in a regression model. For example, consider an employee's job satisfaction measured using four ordered values: 1 = very dissatisfied, 2 = dissatisfied, 3 = satisfied, and 4 = very satisfied. This variable has more than two categories, and thus it is not dichotomous. It also is not an interval-level variable, because there is no good reason to believe that a one-unit difference on the scale always reflects the same difference in job satisfaction as any other one-unit difference. For instance, the difference in satisfaction between individuals with scores of 1 ("very dissatisfied") and 2 ("dissatisfied") is not necessarily the same as the difference in satisfaction between individuals with scores of 2 ("dissatisfied") and 3 ("satisfied"). Although the four values of job satisfaction are expressed as numbers, the numbers are merely convenient symbols for the four levels of satisfaction and are not meant to convey information about the differences between the four scale values. This does not always deter researchers from including a variable like the job satisfaction scale as an independent variable in regression analysis. Yet researchers should understand that when they do so, they are implicitly assuming that each increase of one point on the scale (from 1 to 2, from 2 to 3, and from 3 to 4) reflects the same increase in satisfaction.

Assumption 2: The dependent variable is continuous. Continuous variables are interval-level variables that are free to take on any numerical value. Thus, the number of children in a family would not be continuous, because it is restricted to a small number of integer values (0, 1, 2, 3, . . .); it cannot be 2.46, for example. Measurement constraints serve to prevent *any* variable from being truly continuous, since even a theoretically continuous variable must be rounded off when measured, but some variables are close enough to being continuous that they can easily be treated as such. For example, annual income measured to the nearest thousand dollars (or even the nearest dollar) cannot assume *any* value, but most regression analysts would be comfortable treating income measured in this unit as a continuous variable.

Assumption 3: The variables in the model are measured perfectly (i.e., with no measurement error).   In the body weight illustration, if weights were measured with a bathroom scale, we have to assume that the scale is always accurate; if they were measured through survey responses, we have to assume that people know their own weight and report it truthfully in the survey.

Assumption 4: The effect of the independent variable, X, on the dependent variable, Y, is linear.   Substantively, this means that the strength of the effect of X on Y is the same regardless of the level of X. If this assumption did not hold, it would be inappropriate to characterize the effect of X on Y in a graph by a straight line (i.e., a curve with constant slope). (If the effect of an independent variable on a dependent variable varies with the value of the independent variable, the effect is termed *nonlinear*. Although the basic regression model is linear, some types of nonlinear effects can be specified in a regression using mathematical transformations of the variables in the equation. We discuss this further in Chapter 6.)

Assumption 5: The error or disturbance term is completely uncorrelated with the independent variable.   Recall that the error term represents the effects on the dependent variable of all variables other than the independent variable X, plus any inherent randomness in the process by which Y is determined. Hence the only way we can be confident that the error term is uncorrelated with the independent variable is to believe that any variable (besides the independent variable) that has a substantial influence on the dependent variable is uncorrelated with the independent variable. As you can see, this assumption is extremely demanding. Moreover, assessing whether the assumption is true is difficult, because it involves speculation about numerous variables with *potential* impacts on the dependent variable. In the body weight illustration, if people who eat less tend to be more health conscious and therefore tend to exercise more often, there would be a relationship between food intake and level of exercise; since amount of exercise undoubtedly influences weight, assumption 5 would be violated. But the assumption would also be violated if other variables we have not even thought about influence weight and are correlated with food intake.

In general, assumption 5 is one of several assumptions of regression analysis that together imply that the error term is "random" in its effect on the dependent variable. When you read articles relying on regression, you are likely to come across the terms *heteroscedasticity* and *autocorrelation,* two characteristics of a model's error term that violate the regression assumptions. For now, you need know only that even though heteroscedasticity and autocorrelation have negative consequences for regression analysis (which you will learn about in future courses), when one—or even both—is present, the slope coefficient and the intercept for the regression model still can be interpreted just as if all regression assumptions were satisfied. (In later courses you will learn ways to detect heteroscedasticity and autocorrelation, and techniques to overcome their consequences.)

Because the assumptions of regression are so demanding, and because many assumptions cannot be tested directly—we can only speculate about whether they are met in a particular application of regression—in practice, a researcher can never confidently claim that *all* assumptions of regression have been satisfied completely. In other words, whether an assumption has been satisfied is really a question of degree. When we declare that the regression assumptions have been satisfied for a specific model, we are asserting that there is good reason to believe that the assumptions have been approximately, or roughly, met. Learning how close an approximation is necessary to justify regression analysis is a topic for advanced courses on regression, and a good understanding of it comes only with experience in conducting quantitative analysis.

Estimating Coefficients with Data from a Sample

If the various assumptions of the bivariate regression model have been satisfied, it is appropriate to estimate the slope coefficient and the intercept in the population by (1) selecting a random sample of cases from the population to which the regression equation applies, (2) measuring X and Y for each case in the sample, and then (3) using regression analysis (technically, *ordinary least squares* (OLS) regression) to determine the slope and the intercept of the regression line for the sample. In essence, this calculation involves a mathematical procedure that is the functional equivalent of graphing the X and Y values in a scatterplot and drawing in the line that best "fits" the scattering of points in the graph. Regression analysis, however, identifies the best-fitting line much more effectively than we ever could with mere visual inspection of a scattergram. For instance, consider Figure 2.2, which reproduces the scatterplot of Figure 2.1. It is obvious from just a quick glance that lines 2 and 3 capture the location of the points better than lines 1 and 4. But choosing between lines 2 and 3 on the basis of visual inspection alone is difficult.

In contrast, OLS regression analysis involves a mathematical procedure, generally performed by a computer, that always provides a *unique* best-fitting line. This line is "best" according to a specific definition embodied in the procedure. As its formal name (ordinary *least squares*) suggests, the procedure does the mathematical equivalent of trying all possible lines and identifying the one that *minimizes* the sum of the *squared* vertical distances between the points on the scatterplot and the line.[2] Figure 2.3 reproduces lines 2 and 4 from Figure 2.2. You can see from the graphs that the vertical distances between the points and the line are generally smaller for the better fitting line 2.

---

[2]Recall that the square of a number means the number multiplied by itself [e.g., $8^2 = 8 \times 8 = 64$]. One might alternatively minimize the distances themselves rather than the squared distances. While this procedure would yield nearly the same line as the OLS procedure in most circumstances, there are technical reasons to prefer the regression procedure's attention to squared vertical distances.

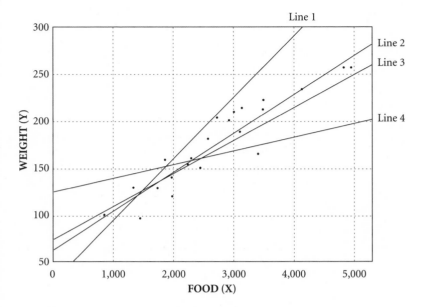

FIGURE 2.2   Which is the best-fitting line?

When you study regression analysis in later course work, you will learn about several desirable statistical properties of the OLS procedure that justify its use. For now, what is important is that if the regression assumptions are met and data for **X** and **Y** for a random sample from a population are available, the values of the slope coefficient and the intercept *in the sample* can be viewed as reasonable *estimates* of their values in the full population. (This is much the same as in an experiment, when we use a random sample to make inferences about the larger population from which the sample was drawn.) Thus, the sample coefficients often are referred to as the *intercept estimate* and the *slope coefficient estimate.*

Although the intercept and slope coefficient estimates can be viewed as reasonable estimates of the true values of the coefficients in the population (*if* the assumptions of regression analysis have been met), there is never good reason to believe that estimates from a sample match their values in the population exactly. Consider Figure 2.4, which again reproduces the scatterplot from Figure 2.1. The solid line in Figure 2.4 is the "true" regression line

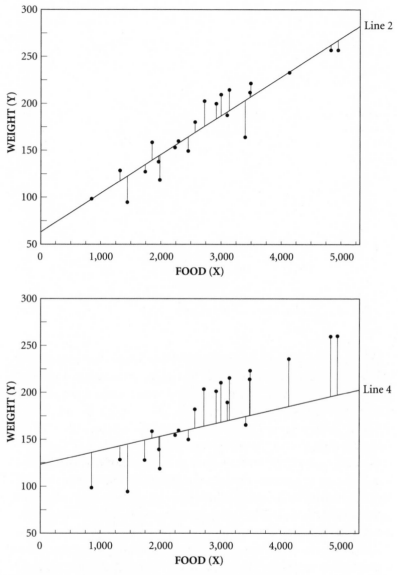

FIGURE 2.3   Vertical distances between points and two lines

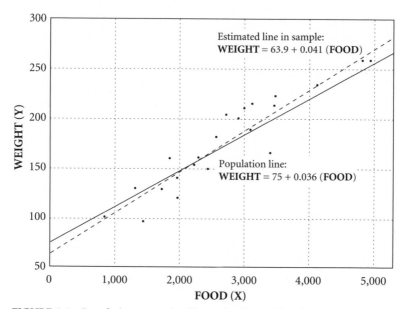

FIGURE 2.4   Population regression line and estimated line based on a sample

for the population, and the dashed line is the sample regression line—the line estimated for the population by applying the OLS regression procedure to the sample of 22 cases.[3] Even though the estimated line is the best-fitting line for the scatterplot and is close to the true line, the intercept and the slope of the true and estimated lines do not correspond exactly.

Nevertheless, statisticians have proved that when the regression assumptions are satisfied, the intercept and slope coefficient estimates are *unbiased;* by this they mean that if we repeated the OLS procedure on a large number of random samples from the population, the coefficient estimates we obtained would, *on average,* equal their true values in the population. In some samples, an estimate would be too high, and in others, too low; but *on average,* the estimates would be on target. Unfortunately, we never know

---

[3]Recall that, in practice, we can never know the true regression line in the population. Indeed, if we knew the line, we would not need to estimate its intercept and slope coefficient using OLS regression and data from a sample.

whether the specific sample we are using is one in which the estimate is too high or too low. This is the inherent limitation of not being able to observe all the cases in the population of interest. Nonetheless, the most critical piece of information produced by a bivariate regression is the slope coefficient estimate, as it is the best available indicator of the impact of X on Y in the population.[4]

---

[4]In some instances, including some of our later examples, researchers have data on the entire population of interest (e.g., all fifty U.S. states). Whether the researcher has data from the entire population or from only a random sample, the slope coefficient estimate remains the best indicator of the impact of X on Y.

3

The Multivariate
Regression Model

The Value of Multivariate Analysis

Although the bivariate regression model is useful for illustrating the technique of regression, it has significant limitations in practical applications. In Chapter 1 we saw that when social scientists claim that a variable, X, influences another variable, Y, they mean that *if all other variables could be held constant,* a change in the value of X will produce a change in the value of Y. The most fundamental limitation of bivariate regression is that it measures the responsiveness of Y to a change in X *without providing a vehicle for "holding other variables constant."* Consider the body weight illustration. On the hypothesis that food intake influences a person's weight, we developed the bivariate regression model of equation 2.2. Yet we also recognized that the amount of exercise an individual gets influences his or her weight, and we speculated further that food intake and amount of exercise may be negatively related (if health-conscious people are more likely both to watch their diet and to get regular exercise). Assuming that all this is true, if we estimate the slope coefficient for the bivariate model and it shows that a decrease in food consumption is associated with a reduction in weight, we have no way of knowing whether the decrease in weight is the result of the lowered food intake or of the likely accompanying increase in exercise.

What we need to do is to measure the responsiveness of a person's weight to a change in food intake *while holding exercise constant.* Ideally, we would assess the impact of food consumption on weight using an experiment that would allow us to hold not only exercise but also all other variables constant. Another possibility would be to design a nonexperimental study in which we intervene and control both our subjects' food intake and their exercise level; this way, we could vary their food intake but have them do the same amount of exercise.

But what should we do if we are concerned with the confounding nature of exercise in our study but controlling our subjects' food intake and exercise level is not feasible? If we can observe the amount of exercise our subjects get, there is a way around the problem. We could measure weight, food intake, and amount of exercise for each person in the study. Then we could choose one specific level of exercise and confine the analysis to people at this level, comparing the weights of "big eaters" to "small eaters" within this subgroup. If big eaters tend to weigh more than small eaters, differential amounts of exercise cannot possibly be responsible, as level of exercise is constant within this subgroup. Thus, by holding exercise constant, we have eliminated it as a possible explanation for any weight difference observed.

Although the general logic underlying this strategy is sound, there are several weaknesses to the approach. Assuming that amount of exercise is measured as a continuous variable to the nearest calorie expended (and not in some preestablished set of exercise categories), there are bound to be very few people at any one value at which we might choose to fix level of exercise, and therefore probably not enough cases for meaningful empirical analysis. To increase the number of cases for analysis, we could establish a small number of categories for level of exercise (e.g., high, medium, low, and none), thereby grouping people with similar, but not identical, levels in the same category. But this would necessarily introduce measurement error into our analysis, since we would be treating similar, but nonidentical, people as the same. Also, even if the resulting measurement error was not too severe, by restricting our analysis to individuals at just one level of exercise, we would be ignoring valuable information from a large number of cases.

Fortunately, we can overcome the weaknesses of this approach by using regression analysis if we extend the bivariate regression model by adding a second independent variable. Including both food intake and amount of exercise as independent variables in the same regression allows us to combine the information about individuals having different levels of exercise to see how weight changes if food intake is increased when amount of exercise is held constant at *any* level. If we extend the model further by adding other variables believed to influence body weight, we can determine how weight changes when food consumption is increased and numerous other variables are held constant.

Interpreting the Coefficients of a Multivariate Regression Model

When more than one independent variable is included in a regression model, we refer to the technique as *multivariate* (or *multiple*) regression. For example, consider a regression equation with dependent variable Y and three independent variables—X_1, X_2, and X_3:

(3.1) $$Y_i = b_0 + b_1 X_{1i} + b_2 X_{2i} + b_3 X_{3i} + e_i.$$

This multivariate model captures the idea that each of the three independent variables affects Y; when we interpret such a model, the critical point to keep in mind is that each slope coefficient measures the responsiveness of the dependent variable to a change in the associated independent variable *when the other two independent variables are held constant.*

When we extend the regression model to two or more independent variables, we lose the ability to represent the equation in a graph, as we would need more than the two physical dimensions of a sheet of paper. But the assumptions of the multivariate model and the interpretations of its coefficients parallel those of the bivariate model in every respect. In particular, it would be appropriate to introduce the regression model of equation 3.1 only if we believed, on the basis of a sound theory, that each of X_1, X_2, and X_3 influences Y in some population. The coefficient b_0 is still called the intercept, and its interpretation is a natural extension of the intercept in bivariate regression: it is the expected (or average) value of **Y** for a case having a score of zero on *each* of the independent variables. The rest of the "b" coefficients in the equation are now called *partial* slope coefficients (or sometimes just slope coefficients); the partial slope coefficient for each of the (three) independent variables is interpreted as the change in the expected (or average) value of **Y** resulting from a one-unit increase in that independent variable when the other (two) independent variables are held constant. Finally, **e** is still called the error (or disturbance) term and again represents the net impact of all variables influencing **Y** that are not included in the equation plus any inherent randomness in the process by which **Y** is determined. We can extend this model to include any number of variables, adding X_4, X_5, and so on, until we have included all the variables that we think have substantial effects on **Y**. This capacity to include numerous independent variables is an important benefit of multiple regression, since most phenomena of interest have multiple causes.

For example, suppose we added amount of exercise (**EXERCISE**) to the bivariate regression model explaining a person's weight to create the following multivariate model:

(3.2) $\text{WEIGHT}_i = b_0 + b_1(\text{FOOD}_i) + b_2(\text{EXERCISE}_i) + e_i.$

As before, **FOOD** is measured as average daily food consumption in calories during the year prior to the observation of weight; similarly, we measure **EXERCISE** as average daily energy expenditure, also in calories. Assume that the intercept, b_0, is 152 and that the partial slope coefficients are (for **FOOD**) $b_1 = 0.028$ and (for **EXERCISE**) $b_2 = -0.045$. The identical information is presented in a different form in Table 3.1. (Such tables are a common way of reporting regression coefficients in the social sciences.) [!! *Try to interpret the meaning of the intercept and partial slope coefficients in Table 3.1.*]

The intercept can be interpreted as the expected weight of a person who consumes no food and expends no energy, but, as with our bivariate model, the intercept has no substantive meaning, because the type of person described is nonexistent. We can, however, use the intercept and partial slope coefficient estimates to calculate the expected value of **WEIGHT** at any given levels of

TABLE 3.1   Regression Coefficients for Multivariate Model Explaining Body Weight

	Coefficient Symbol	Population Coefficient
Intercept	b_0	152.000
FOOD	b_1	0.028
EXERCISE	b_2	− 0.045

FOOD and **EXERCISE**. For example, someone whose daily food consumption is 3,200 calories and whose daily energy expenditure is 1,800 calories has an expected weight of 160.6 pounds, because $152 + (0.028 \times 3,200) - (0.045 \times 1,800) = 160.6$.

The partial slope coefficients enable us to characterize the responsiveness of the dependent variable to a change in each independent variable when the other independent variable is held constant. The coefficient b_1 can be interpreted as the change in expected weight associated with a one-unit increase in food intake *while holding the level of exercise constant;* similarly, b_2 describes the response of expected weight to a one-unit increase in exercise *when the level of food intake is held constant.* Thus, the slope coefficient of 0.028 (for **FOOD**) indicates that an increase of 100 calories in average daily intake is associated with an increase in expected weight of 2.8 (i.e., 100×0.028) pounds when amount of exercise is held constant at any value. Similarly, the slope coefficient for **EXERCISE** implies that when food intake is fixed at any level, an increase of 100 calories in average daily energy expenditure results in an average weight decrease of 4.5 (i.e., 100×-0.045) pounds.

Dichotomous and Categorical Independent Variables

As with the bivariate regression model, the multivariate model requires that independent variables be interval level or dichotomous (i.e., restricted to only two values). The interpretation of the partial slope coefficient for a variable is the same whether the variable is dichotomous or interval level. However, the custom in the social sciences is for the two values of a dichotomous variable to be labeled 0 and 1,[1] which allows the interpretation of the slope coefficient to be stated in an especially simple way. We need only recognize that when a variable must be either 0 or 1, a one-unit increase can only mean one thing: a change from one category of the variable (the one scored zero) to the other. No other unit increase is possible. Thus, when X_1 is dichotomous and scored 0 or 1, the partial slope coefficient, b_1, can be interpreted as the difference in the expected value of Y between a case for which $X_1 = 0$ and a case for which $X_1 = 1$ (when the cases have identical values on all other independent variables).

For example, suppose we believed that what sex a person is has some bearing on his or her weight, leading us to amend our regression model for weight (equation 3.2) by adding the dichotomous independent variable **MALE**, which we set as 1 for males and 0 for females:

$$\text{WEIGHT}_i = b_0 + b_1(\text{FOOD}_i) + b_2(\text{EXERCISE}_i) + b_3(\text{MALE}_i) + e_i.$$

Assume that the slope coefficient (b_3) for sex is 35. [!! *Interpret the meaning of the slope coefficient, 35, for the variable MALE.*] This means that if two individuals, one male and one female, have identical levels of food consumption and exercise, then the man can be expected to weigh 35 pounds more than the woman.

Sometimes researchers are interested in assessing the effect of a *categorical* independent variable on a dependent variable. Categorical variables (sometimes called *nominal, qualitative,* or *discrete*) are variables that take on three or more values (or categories) but are not measured at the interval level. The values can have either a clear ordering (e.g., a variable measuring an individual's response to a survey statement as "strongly disagree," "disagree," "agree," or "strongly agree") or no substantively meaningful order (e.g., the region in which an individual lives— Northeast, Midwest, Southeast, etc.). Although assumption 1 precludes using a categorical variable directly in a regression

---

[1]The specific labels used to represent the two values are arbitrary in the sense that the conclusions from regression analysis are completely unaffected by what labels are used.

model as an independent variable, the impact of such a variable can be specified by using a series of dichotomous variables. The trick is to use precisely one dichotomous variable less than the number of categories the variable can assume. (You will learn the reasoning behind this procedure when you take a course on regression analysis.)

For instance, suppose we believe that a four-category independent variable, X_1, influences a dependent variable, Y. We label the four categories c, d, e, and f (which could represent four regions of the United States, or four responses to a survey question). To incorporate the effect of X_1 on Y in a regression model, three dichotomous variables would be constructed, each of which would equal 1 when X_1 equals one of its four values, and 0 when X_1 takes any of the other three values. We could let

$$C_i = 1 \text{ if } X_{1i} = c, \text{ and } C_i = 0 \text{ otherwise;}$$

$$D_i = 1 \text{ if } X_{1i} = d, \text{ and } D_i = 0 \text{ otherwise; and}$$

$$E_i = 1 \text{ if } X_{1i} = e, \text{ and } E_i = 0 \text{ otherwise.}$$

With this scoring system, the "missing" value of X_1—namely f—is described as the "reference category."[2] To specify that X_1 influences Y, the three dichotomous variables are included in a regression equation along with other independent variables (say, X_4 and X_5) that influence Y:

$$Y_i = b_0 + b_1 C_i + b_2 D_i + b_3 E_i + b_4 X_{4i} + b_5 X_{5i} + e_i.$$

It turns out that the slope coefficient for each of the dichotomous variables (C, D, or E) can be interpreted as the difference in the expected value of Y between a case in the associated category of X_1 (c, d, or e) and a case in the reference category, f, when the cases have

---

[2]The category chosen to be the reference category is arbitrary; it does not affect the interpretation of the regression model.

identical values on the other independent variables. For example, the coefficient b_1 for C is the difference in the expected value of Y between a case for which $X_1 = c$ and a case having the same values for X_4 and X_5 but for which $X_1 = f$. (When you study regression analysis, you will learn why the coefficients for the dichotomous variables can be given this sort of special interpretation.)

Consider once again our body weight model of equation 3.2. Suppose that we are not able to measure the variable **EXERCISE** (recall that this variable measures average daily energy expenditure, in calories), but that we do have information about the occupations of the individuals being studied. We might use occupational data as a substitute (or proxy) for a direct measure of exercise. Specifically, we could categorize individuals into three groups based on their primary job context: (1) those who have desk jobs, (2) those who engage in light labor (e.g., cashiers, clerks), and (3) those who engage in heavy physical labor. If we believed that individuals in these different categories get differing amounts of exercise when performing their jobs, then occupation would be a categorical variable hypothesized to influence the dependent variable **WEIGHT**. We would arbitrarily establish one of the three categories of the variable (say "desk job") as the "reference" category and then construct two dichotomous variables:

LIGHTWORK$_i$ equals 1 if individual *i* engages in light labor, and 0 otherwise; and

HEAVYWORK$_i$ equals 1 if individual *i* engages in heavy labor, and 0 otherwise.

Assume that these two variables were included in the place of **EXERCISE** in equation 3.2, and that the partial slope coefficients for **LIGHTWORK** and **HEAVYWORK** were –6 and –18, respectively. [!! *Try to interpret the meaning of the slope coefficients –6 and –18.*] This would imply that the expected weight of a light laborer is 6 pounds less than the expected weight of a desk worker with an identical level of food intake. Similarly, the average weight of a heavy laborer is 18 pounds less than the expected weight of a desk worker who has the same level of food consumption. Note that these results also imply that a heavy laborer should, on average, weigh 12 pounds less than a light laborer. (This is computed by subtracting the coefficient for **LIGHTWORK** from that for **HEAVYWORK**: $-18 - (-6) = -12$.)

The Assumptions of Multivariate Regression

The assumptions of the multivariate regression model are natural extensions of the assumptions of the bivariate model. Assumption 2—that the dependent variable is continuous—remains unchanged, and the other regression assumptions must now be satisfied for each independent variable. Thus, all independent variables must be either interval level or dichotomous (assumption 1); all variables in the model must be measured without error (assumption 3); the effect of each independent variable on the dependent variable must be linear (assumption 4); and the error term must be completely uncorrelated with each independent variable (assumption 5). The last of these assumptions is very demanding; to be confident that it holds, one must believe that *any* variable that has a significant effect on the dependent variable but is not included among the independent variables must be unrelated to *all* included independent variables. Therefore, just as with bivariate regression, analysts using multiple regression must consider the likely effects of variables not included in the model.

An additional assumption, unique to the multivariate model, is also required:

Assumption 6: The effects of all independent variables on the dependent variable are additive.   Two independent variables are said to have additive effects on Y if the effect of each is the same regardless of the value of the other. (In contrast, we say that two variables *interact* in influencing Y if the effect of one on Y varies with the value of the other. We discuss "interaction" further and provide an example in Chapter 6.) Table 3.2 lists all the assumptions of the multivariate regression model discussed in this book.

As with bivariate regression, if the multivariate regression assumptions are met in a substantive application, it is appropriate to draw a random sample of cases from the population of interest,

TABLE 3.2   Some Assumptions of Multivariate Regression

1. All independent variables are measured at the interval level, or are dichotomous.
2. The dependent variable is continuous.
3. All variables in the model are measured perfectly (i.e., with no measurement error).
4. The effect of each independent variable on the dependent variable is linear.
5. The error term is completely uncorrelated with each independent variable.
6. The effects of all independent variables on the dependent variable are additive.

NOTE: Some assumptions of regression analysis are beyond the scope of this book and are not listed here.

measure all variables for each case, and use regression analysis to estimate the intercept and each of the partial slope coefficients on the basis of data from the sample.

Choosing the Independent Variables for a Regression Model

The choice of the independent variables to include in a regression model is of critical importance in applied research, largely for two reasons. First, as we saw in the previous section, if we are to avoid violating assumption 5, any variable that has a substantial impact on the dependent variable must either be included in the regression or be uncorrelated with all independent variables that are included. Second, recall that the aim of regression analysis is to measure the responsiveness of the dependent variable to a change in each independent variable while holding the remaining independent variables constant. When an independent variable that influences the dependent variable is excluded from the regression equation, we have no mechanism for holding this variable constant, and hence we cannot accurately measure the effects of the variables that are included. Because the choice of independent variables is so important, researchers writing up their findings for publication typically devote a great deal of attention to explaining and justifying their choices.

Social scientists conducting studies that rely on multiple regression typically defend their choice of independent variables in one of two ways. Sometimes they have a small number of hypotheses of central theoretical interest, thereby justifying the inclusion of a small number of independent variables—say X_1, X_2, and X_3. However, if they are doing thorough research, they do not stop there. They also speculate about other variables that may affect their dependent variable—say Z_1, Z_2, Z_3, and Z_4—and add these variables to the regression model so that the response of Y to changes in X_1, X_2, and X_3, holding the Z variables constant, can be estimated. Here the Zs are included purely for instrumental purposes. The researcher has no direct interest in their effects on the dependent variable but includes them in order to obtain accurate estimates of the effects of the Xs. Thus, in the parlance of research methodology, the Zs are included in the model as *statistical controls.*

Social scientists also may develop multiple regression models by identifying a dependent variable and attempting to develop a theory that can explain changes in the variable as fully as possible. This leads researchers not to focus on a small number of independent variables and treat the rest as statistical controls, but instead to construct a larger set of hypotheses about variables that influence their dependent variable. Collectively these hypotheses are thought to constitute an explanation for changes in the dependent variable. The explanation is then tested by including the independent variables associated with each hypothesis in a multivariate regression model. With this approach, the author does not think explicitly about what variables must be included in the regression as statistical controls, yet statistical control is nonetheless accomplished, as each partial slope coefficient estimate measures the response of Y to a change in an independent variable when all other independent variables in the model are held constant.

4

Evaluating Regression Results

Standardized Coefficients

The partial slope coefficients we have been examining are often referred to as *unstandardized* coefficients; they are coefficients that measure the effects of variables expressed in the original units of measurement. Sometimes coefficients are reported in a different form as *standardized* coefficients (or *beta weights*). The precise meaning of standardized coefficients cannot be understood without some background in statistics. But the basic goal of using standardized coefficients is to be able to compare the relative effects on a dependent variable of multiple independent variables measured in different units. The idea is to transform the measurement units of all independent variables in a regression model to a common unit (hence, to *standardize* the variables), so that if the standardized coefficient for one variable is 0.40 and the standardized coefficient for another is 0.20, the impact of the first can be said to be twice as strong as that of the second regardless of their different original units of measurement.

For example, in an article in the *American Sociological Review,* Catherine E. Ross and Chia-ling Wu (1995) measure the effects of various factors on the self-reported health of American adults. These factors include *exercise* (measured as the frequency with which one engages in various forms of physical exercise) and *education* (measured by the number of years of schooling), both of which are expected to have positive effects on health, as well as *age,* measured in years, which is expected to have a negative impact. Someone reading this study might ask, "Which of these three independent variables has the strongest impact on health?" Clearly, unstandardized slope coefficients do not help to answer this question, since the three variables have different measurement scales. Even for the two variables that are measured in the same unit—education and age, in years—a one-unit increase probably does not mean the same thing. Since the age of adults varies from 21 to over 90 (for a range of 70 years or more), but years of schooling has a maximum of about 20, one year of schooling probably should be viewed as a "larger" increase than one year of age. To overcome this interpretation problem, Ross and Wu report standardized slope coefficients for the variables: –0.205 for age, 0.091 for education, and 0.088 for exercise. These values imply that exercise and education have roughly equal effects on health and that the effect of age is more than twice as strong as either of them.

However, a reliance on standardized regression coefficients to make this kind of comparative assessment is justifiable only if one has confidence that the differing scales of measurement for the independent variables have indeed been converted to a common scale. Making this case requires some very strong assumptions about how the values of each of the independent variables are spread across cases, and in most situations it will not be evident that these assumptions can reasonably be made. (Note that it should not be obvious to you why this makes sense; understanding the rationale for this claim requires some background in statistics.) For this reason, we believe that standardized coefficients are overused in the social sciences. Our advice is to downplay the importance of interpretations of standardized regression coefficients in studies you read, and to focus greater attention on characterizing the magnitude of the effect of each independent variable separately (and in its natural unit) through an analysis of unstandardized coefficients. Fortunately, even if an author emphasizes the interpretation of standardized coefficients in the text, in most studies (including the Ross and Wu article), the unstandardized coefficients are also reported in tables, and readers are free to draw their own interpretations from these values.

Strong Relationships Among the Independent Variables: The Problem of Multicollinearity

As we have seen, multivariate regression enables researchers to estimate the effects of several independent variables on a dependent variable. How well regression can do this is partially determined by the strength of the relationships *among* the independent variables. The presence of relationships among the independent variables in a regression model is known as *multicollinearity*. There will be *some* multicollinearity in virtually every regression model, but if the relationships among the independent variables are not strong, the OLS regression procedure for estimating slope coefficients can proceed without difficulty. Yet strong multicollinearity is not at all unusual in social science research. For example, sociologists have hypothesized that many attitudes of individuals are influenced by both their level of education and their family income. Since education is an important determinant of income, the two variables are strongly related, and a model including both variables is likely to be characterized by substantial multicollinearity.

Strong multicollinearity poses serious problems for regression analysis. To see why, we return to our body weight example. Suppose we added the independent variable fat intake measured in grams (denoted **FAT**) to the model that already includes food intake measured in calories (**FOOD**). These two variables are conceptually distinct. For example, some foods are low in fat but high in sugar, and thus contain many calories. Still, in a typical group of persons, fat intake and total calorie consumption will be strongly correlated, with big eaters tending to consume more fat than small eaters. The difficulty for regression is that because food consumption and fat intake are highly correlated, they are "competing" to explain the same variation in body weight, and the OLS procedure has difficulty allocating explanatory power between these two variables. If one of them predicts weight well, so will the other.

Another way to think about the problem is as follows. In the regression, the partial slope coefficient for **FOOD** represents the change in weight associated with a one-unit increase in **FOOD** when **FAT** is held constant. However, if food consumption and fat intake are highly correlated, then the scenario of "increasing food consumption while holding fat intake constant" is purely hypothetical. In fact, when food consumption increases across subjects in the sample, fat intake will increase as well. This means that the data from the sample will offer very little information about what happens when food consumption increases *while fat intake remains unchanged*—which makes it difficult to estimate the effect of food intake on weight. (In future courses you will learn how to diagnose multicollinearity, and some ways to work around this problem.)

Measuring the Fit of a Regression Model

In the bivariate regression model, the OLS regression procedure enables researchers to find the line that best fits the scatterplot for the relationship between X and Y. In the multivariate model, we can no longer talk about a best-fitting *line* (because the regression equation can no longer be represented by a line), but it remains true that the OLS procedure finds the coefficient estimates that provide the "best fit" with the data. However, an obvious question remains: The fit may be the best possible, but how good is it? The answer is based on a comparison between *actual* and *predicted* values of Y.

Suppose OLS regression for a two-independent variable model generates the sample equation

$$Y_i = 6 + 8X_{1i} - 3X_{2i}.$$

This equation yields a predicted value of Y for each case in the sample. Take a case for which $X_1 = 2$, $X_2 = 5$, and $Y = 12$. The regression equation predicts that this case has a Y value of 7 (since $6 + (8 \times 2) - (3 \times 5) = 7$). Yet its actual Y value is 12. Thus, there is a deviation of 5 (i.e., $12 - 7$) between actual and predicted values of Y. If the deviation between actual and predicted Y values were zero for all cases, the regression equation would have a perfect fit with the data; as these deviations get larger, the degree of fit declines.

The most commonly reported measure of fit for a bivariate or multivariate regression model is R^2 (pronounced "*R-squared*"). There are several definitions of R^2 that are mathematically equivalent, and when you take a class on regression you will learn what these are and why they are equivalent. For now it is sufficient to understand that R^2 is equal to the *square* of the *correlation* between the *actual* values of **Y** and the *predicted* values of **Y** for the cases in the sample. Since correlation coefficients run from −1 to 1, and since the square of any number (including a negative number) is positive, R^2 is always between 0 and 1. Here too, the higher the value, the better the fit, and a value of 1 indicates a perfect fit. The most common interpretation you will see for R^2 in published research is that it represents the proportion of the variation in **Y** that is explained by the independent variables in the model. (When you take a course on regression analysis, you will learn why R^2 can be interpreted in this way.) Low values for R^2 mean that the independent variables have little explanatory power, and higher values indicate greater explanatory power.

Statistical Significance

When you study regression analysis at a more advanced level, you will learn how to tell whether the partial slope coefficient estimate for an independent variable in a regression equation is *statistically significant*. The precise meaning of this term cannot be understood without some background in inferential statistics. But fundamentally, the interest in statistical significance reflects a recognition that in any random sample from a population, the relationships between the independent and the dependent variables are not exactly the same as the relationships between them in the population. Indeed, some samples are unusual enough in their character that relationships appear in the sample even when there are *no* relationships in the underlying population. Just as the scattering of stars in the night sky may, in some circumstances, appear to take the form of a familiar object, sometimes in a particular sample the unlikely does happen, and a nonrelationship appears to be a relationship. The concept of statistical significance helps us to express a degree of confidence that a relationship we detect is more than a chance occurrence in the one sample that we are able to observe.

One way to think about this is as follows: A partial slope coefficient estimate provides information about the relationship between variables in the specific sample on which the regression analysis is conducted. Because the values of the error terms for cases vary from one sample of a population to another, the partial slope coefficient estimate for an independent variable varies across samples, and in any one sample it may be higher or lower than the true value of the coefficient in the population. Of course, generally, we are more interested in the value of a partial slope coefficient in the population than in its value in a single sample, and thus we infer information about the value of a population coefficient from its value in the sample. When we conduct a test of statistical significance, the point is to avoid assigning substantive meaning to a relationship that, although present in a particular sample, does not exist in the full population.

A test of statistical significance for a partial slope coefficient estimate usually involves the following question: How likely is it that a researcher would observe a partial slope coefficient estimate of the magnitude found in the *sample* if the true slope coefficient in the *population* were zero? Authors often report that some partial slope coefficient estimate—call it $b_{1(est)}$ (for the coefficient for X_1)—is statistically significant at the 5 percent level (or, equivalently, at the .05 level). By this they mean that statistical theory tells them that *if* the true (population) value of b_1 *were zero* (and thus X_1 actually had *no effect* on Y), then a random sample from the population could be expected to yield an estimate of b_1 at least as large as the observed estimate less frequently than 5 times out of 100 (which is what is meant by the 5 percent level). Therefore, obtaining an estimate as large as $b_{1(est)}$ would be very unlikely if b_1 were actually zero. But $b_{1(est)}$ *was* obtained. As a result, the hypothesis that the population coefficient b_1 equals zero is rejected in favor of the assertion that it is different from zero. Note that this is not proof that the population value is different from zero, just an assertion that this is very likely so.[1] Note also that a separate determination of statistical significance applies to each partial slope co-

---

[1] It is common practice in the social sciences to conduct tests of statistical significance even when the researcher does regression analysis using all cases in the population. In such situations, the concept of statistical significance has a slightly different interpretation (which can be understood only after studying statistics).

efficient in a regression model. Thus it is possible that the coefficients for some independent variables prove to be statistically significant while the coefficients for others are not significant.

It is standard practice for social scientists to present evidence concerning the statistical significance of their coefficient estimates alongside the estimates themselves. They may do so in a number of different ways. Researchers may report each slope coefficient's *standard error.* Although this is a concept that cannot be understood without some background in statistics, the key to interpreting a standard error is to recognize that it is used in conjunction with the associated slope coefficient estimate to determine the coefficient's statistical significance. A rule of thumb—not exactly accurate, but close—is that a coefficient estimate is statistically significant at the .05 level if it is more than twice the size of its standard error, in either the positive or negative direction.

Alternatively, researchers may present a *t-statistic* (also called a *t-ratio* or *t-score*) for each slope coefficient estimate, which is simply the coefficient value divided by its standard error. The rule of thumb presented above implies that one can say that a coefficient is statistically significant at the .05 level if the corresponding *t*-statistic is greater than 2 or less than −2.

Although the .05 level is a widely accepted standard, or cutoff level, for statistical significance, researchers may use a criterion that is more liberal (say, the .10 level, accepting a lower *t*-statistic of lower magnitude as significant) or more conservative (say, the .01 level, requiring a higher *t*-statistic of greater magnitude). The lower the cutoff level for statistical significance, the more confident we can be that the associated population coefficient is not zero. Sometimes researchers report what is termed the *p-value* for a slope coefficient estimate. This is the *precise* probability (as opposed to a cutoff level) that a random sample from the population would yield a slope estimate at least as large as the observed estimate *if* the true population slope coefficient were equal to zero. Thus, the smaller the *p*-value, the greater the confidence we can have that the population slope coefficient being estimated is different from zero.

Finally, in conjunction with any of the above approaches for reporting results about statistical significance, researchers often mark coefficients that are statistically significant with asterisks and include a note at the bottom of the table indicating the meaning of different numbers of asterisks. This note frequently compares p-values to standard cutoff levels. For example, it may report the following categories:

$$^* p < .05$$
$$^{**} p < .01$$
$$^{***} p < .001$$

Here, one asterisk means that a slope coefficient estimate is statistically significant at the .05 level but not at the .01 level, two asterisks mean significant at the .01 level but not the .001 level, and three asterisks indicate significance at the .001 level. In this usage, more asterisks mean a greater chance that the true slope coefficient in the population is different from zero.

The most important lesson about statistical significance is that there is not necessarily a correspondence between "statistical significance" and "substantive importance." Since tests of statistical significance only provide support for a hypothesis that a partial slope coefficient is different from *zero,* and since a nonzero number can still be small, "statistically significant" should not be viewed as synonymous with "substantively strong."

For example, suppose a partial slope coefficient estimate indicates that an increase of 100 calories in average daily food intake results in an increase in expected body weight of one-tenth of a pound. Even if this coefficient estimate were statistically significant, we would not want to view the estimated effect of food consumption on weight as *substantively* important, since the estimated response of weight to an appreciable increase in caloric consumption is trivially small.

Yet even people trained in statistics sometimes make the mistake of equating "statistically significant" with "substantively strong." You should learn now to avoid this error. Especially in a large sample, a partial slope coefficient estimate that is statistically significant may indicate a weak impact (in substantive terms). Consequently, even after you learn much more about tests of statistical significance, the most critical information you use to judge the magnitude of the effect of an independent variable should still be the size of its partial slope coefficient esti-mate evaluated in the context of the measurement scales for the variables involved.

Cross-Sectional vs. Time-Series Data

All the regression examples presented so far involve *cross-sectional* data, that is, data collected by observing the values of the variables for multiple cases at a single point in time. For instance, in all our illustrations involving food and weight, we have assumed that we observe each person in a sample once and at the same time. In other situations, regression models are estimated with *time-series* data, which are based on observations of a single unit at multiple time points. For example, Kiser and Drass (1987) use time-series regression to test a variety of hypotheses about variables influenc-ing the rate of production of utopian novels in the United States (i.e., the number of utopian novels published divided by the total number of books published) over the period of 1883–1975. They collect the data for their regression model by measuring all vari-ables in each year between 1883 and 1975, thereby producing 93 cases for analysis.

Scholars also may estimate coefficients for a regression model with data that are neither purely cross-sectional nor purely time-series, but rather consist of observations drawn from multiple cases over multiple time periods; such data are sometimes referred to as *pooled* data. For instance, Kone and Winters (1993) test the hypothesis that the enactment of sales and income taxes influences the outcome of elections for governor using regression analysis on pooled data, in which the cases are all states in years between 1957 and 1985 in which a gubernatorial election was held.

Time-series and pooled data tend to create statistical problems different from those of cross-sectional data, and often these prob-lems lead researchers to modify the OLS regression procedure used to estimate slope coefficients and information about statisti-cal significance. You may see references to generalized least squares (GLS), least squares dummy variables (LSDV), panel cor-rected standard errors (PCSE), or other procedures when reading articles involving time-series or pooled data. You will learn more about these methods in future course work. For now, though, what is important to know is that the estimation procedure does not affect the interpretation of the partial slope coefficient estimates. Regardless of the technique used to derive coefficient estimates, they can be interpreted just as though they had been obtained by the standard OLS procedure.

5

Some Illustrations of
Multiple Regression

Lobbying in Congress

In an article in the *American Political Science Review,* John Wright
(1990) uses multiple regression analysis to test a set of hypotheses
about the factors influencing the extent to which members of the
U.S. House of Representatives are lobbied by interest groups. (Recall that *lobbying* refers to attempts by individuals and groups to
influence government officials.) The issue Wright studies for this
analysis is the consideration of the reauthorization of the 1980
legislation, the Comprehensive Environmental Response, Com-
pensation, and Liability Act (i.e., the "Superfund"), by the 36
members of the House Ways and Means Committee in 1985.
Specifically, he focuses on lobbying activity directed at the committee concerning the question of "who would pay for hazardous
waste cleanup. . . . [This] question split the business community
between oil and chemical producers [. . . which favored a broad-
based tax], and a broad base of general businesses on the other
hand [. . . which supported a] plan to concentrate the tax burden
on the oil and chemical industry" (p. 420).

Wright's hypotheses lead him to propose the following regression model:

(5.1)   **LOBBYING GROUPS**$_i$ = b$_0$ + b$_1$**IDEOLOGY**$_i$ +
        b$_2$**REPUBLICAN**$_i$ + b$_3$**LEADER**$_i$ +
        b$_4$**CONSTITUENCY STRENGTH**$_i$ +
        b$_5$**CONTRIBUTING GROUPS**$_i$ +
        b$_6$**$ CONTRIBUTED**$_i$ + e$_i$.

The variables are defined as follows: **LOBBYING GROUPS**$_i$ denotes "the number of groups lobbying [representative *i*] for passage of the [bill adopting a broad-based tax]." **IDEOLOGY**$_i$ represents ideology measured on a conservative-liberal continuum by
the Americans for Democratic Action (ADA) score for representative *i*; it is coded so that more liberal representatives receive higher
scores.[1] **REPUBLICAN**$_i$ is a dichotomous variable indicating the
representative's political party affiliation; Democrats are coded 0
and Republicans 1. **LEADER**$_i$, also a dichotomous variable, indicates "whether the representative is a committee leader" (0 = no, 1
= yes). **CONSTITUENCY STRENGTH**$_i$ reflects the strength of
the oil and chemical industry in representative *i*'s constituency, as
measured by "the total value added (in millions of dollars) by producers of petroleum and chemical products within [*i*'s] district."
CONTRIBUTING GROUPS$_i$ is "the total   ber of groups [sup-
porting a broad-based tax] that made a campaign contribution to
the representative during the 1983–84 election cycle." **$ CON-
TRIBUTED**$_i$ is the amount contributed to representative *i* (in
thousands of dollars) by groups supporting a broad-based tax minus the amount contributed by groups against the broad-based
tax.[2] Finally, e$_i$ is a disturbance term.

(Since regression analysis is appropriate only when there is a
sound theory suggesting why the independent variables in the regression equation should influence the dependent variable, a critical evaluation of research relying on regression should always be-

---

[1]The Americans for Democratic Action is a liberal interest group that assigns
ratings to members of Congress on the degree to which they support legislation
of importance to the group.

[2]Wright's article incorrectly states that **$ CONTRIBUTED** is measured in dol-
lars (rather than thousands of dollars). He acknowledges the error in written
correspondence.

gin with an assessment of the theory underlying the model. However, since our purpose here is not to evaluate the quality of Wright's research, we present very little of the theory that Wright introduces to justify his regression model. Interested readers should refer to the original article for Wright's full defense.)

Wright recognizes that one of the important assumptions of the regression model may be violated in this application: assumption 5—that the error term is uncorrelated with each of the independent variables. For Wright's model, groups on the other side of the issue may constitute a problem. If interest groups lobby partly to counteract the influence of groups on the other side, then the variable "number of groups lobbying *against* passage of the bill" would be part of the error term, as it would be a factor that influences the dependent variable (number of groups lobbying *for* passage) but is excluded from the regression model. The issue then would be whether "number of groups lobbying against" is unrelated to each of the independent variables in equation 5.1. And the very same reasoning (underlying the regression) that suggests that these independent variables influence "the number of groups lobbying for" would suggest that these variables are also related to "number of groups lobbying against." Wright ultimately justifies the use of regression analysis in his study despite this line of reasoning by noting that "there is little or no available theory about whether or when groups might lobby in order to counteract the influence of other groups" (p. 423). Of course, readers can and should judge for themselves whether this argument is convincing. (When you study regression analysis in greater depth, you will learn more about the consequences for coefficient estimates of violating assumption 5 as well as the other regression assumptions. If you find Wright's logic unconvincing, a knowledge of the consequences would help you to assess the seriousness of the violation of the assumption.)

What about the other regression assumptions? All of Wright's independent variables are either dichotomous or measured at the interval level, and thus assumption 1 has been met. As for assumption 2, most researchers would probably deem it reasonable to view **LOBBYING GROUPS** as approximately continuous, despite the fact that it is restricted to integers, because of the variable's wide range (Wright indicates that **LOBBYING GROUPS** can be any integer between 0 and 24).

The certainty that variables have been measured without error (assumption 3) varies from one variable to another. Unless there were clerical errors in recording information, party affiliation (**REPUBLICAN**) should be measured perfectly, since such affiliations are a matter of public record. Assessing the quality of measurement of **IDEOLOGY** is more controversial. The ADA score is a widely used measure of ideology in the political science literature, but that is no guarantee that it is perfect. In addition to any questions we might have about clerical errors (e.g., as Wright entered ADA scores for his data set or as the ADA counted legislators' votes when constructing its rankings), a careful evaluation of measurement error would also consider whether the ADA selected issues that provide a reliable gauge of the liberal-conservative dimension when developing its rating system for the year of analysis.

Finally, are the effects of variables in equation 5.1 linear (assumption 4) and additive (assumption 6), as required by the regression model? Wright presents no theory that would suggest that these assumptions have been violated, but readers should do their own theorizing. To evaluate the soundness of the linearity and additivity assumptions, readers should ask themselves, for each independent variable, whether the impact of the variable on the number of groups lobbying for passage should vary with the value of (1) that independent variable (for the linearity assumption) or (2) the other independent variables in the model (for the additivity assumption).

Using data for all 36 members of the Ways and Means Committee, Wright obtained the coefficient estimates reported in Table 5.1 using OLS regression. Wright's model has an R^2 value of 0.51. [!! *R^2 was discussed in Chapter 4. Try to interpret the meaning of the R^2 value of 0.51.*] This indicates that the variables Wright included in his model together explain 51 percent of the variation in the extent to which members of Congress were lobbied by interest groups in favor of the broad-based tax.

[!! *Recall the rule of thumb that a slope coefficient is statistically significant at the .05 level if the associated t-statistic is greater than 2 or less than –2. Use the t-statistic values in Table 5.1 to determine*

TABLE 5.1   Wright's Model of Lobbying

	Population Coefficient	Coefficient Estimate	t-statistic
Intercept	b_0	12.82**	5.42
IDEOLOGY	b_1	−0.10**	−3.31
REPUBLICAN	b_2	−3.38*	−1.62
LEADER	b_3	3.16**	2.35
CONSTITUENCY STRENGTH	b_4	0.30	0.48
CONTRIBUTING GROUPS	b_5	0.69*	1.45
$ CONTRIBUTED	b_6	−0.23	−0.58

$R^2 = 0.51$.

  * Statistically significant at .10 level.
** Statistically significant at .05 level.

SOURCE: Table 1 from Wright 1990.

which independent variables have coefficients that are statistically significant at the .05 level.] However, as shown in Table 5.1 by the use (or omission) of asterisks, not all of the slope coefficients in Wright's model achieve statistical significance. Wright identifies two variables, **CONSTITUENCY STRENGTH** and **$ CONTRIBUTED**, as having statistically insignificant effects. Of the remaining variables, only two—**IDEOLOGY** and **LEADER**—have slope coefficients that are statistically significant at the .05 level. (Note that these are the only two variables that have t-statistics greater than 2 or less than −2.) When presenting his results, Wright notes that these two variables are among the most important predictors of lobbying activity. He also identifies the slope coefficient estimates for two other variables, **REPUBLICAN** and **CONTRIBUTING GROUPS**, as statistically significant. However, their relatively low t-ratios suggest, as Wright acknowledges, that he is using a more liberal standard of statistical significance than the .05 level—namely .10.

[!! *Interpret the meaning of the slope coefficient estimate, −0.10, for IDEOLOGY.*] Wright's results suggest that conservative representatives were lobbied more heavily for the passage of the broad-based tax than were their liberal colleagues. The partial slope coefficient estimate of −0.10 for **IDEOLOGY** indicates that when all other independent variables are held constant, each one-unit increase in the ADA voting score of a member of the House Ways and Means Committee resulted in a decrease of about 0.10 in the expected number of groups lobbying the member for passage of the broad-based tax. Since ADA scores range from 0 (most conservative) to 100 (most liberal), this means that movement along the scale from the most conservative ideology to the most liberal is associated with a reduction of 10 (i.e., 100 × −0.10) in the expected number of groups lobbying a member for passage. An assessment of the strength of this effect is necessarily subjective, but it should be based on a recognition of the measurement scale for the dependent variable. It is clear that a score of zero on the dependent variable is indicative of the lowest possible level of lobbying to which a member can be subjected; less clear is what score would be needed to pass a threshold for "heavy" lobbying activity. In making this judgment, ideally we would know the range in values of the dependent variable across committee members, but Wright did not report this figure. We do know, however, that 24 is the highest possible score that could be assigned for **LOBBYING GROUPS**, since Wright reports that only 24 of the groups studied claimed to have lobbied at least one member. Comparing a value of 10 (the estimated difference between an extreme liberal and an extreme conservative in the expected value of **LOBBYING GROUPS**) to this maximum possible difference of 24 between any two members suggests that the effect of ideology is very strong.

LEADER is a dichotomous variable labeled 1 for committee leaders and 0 otherwise. [!! *Interpret the meaning of the slope coefficient estimate, 3.16, for LEADER.*] The fact that the partial slope coefficient estimate for **LEADER** is positive supports the hypothesis that leaders are subjected to more intense lobbying than are other members. Specifically, a committee leader could have been expected to be lobbied by 3.16 more groups than a nonleader, assuming the two individuals have the same scores on all other independent variables. **REPUBLICAN** is another dichotomous variable—scored 0 for Democrats and 1 for Republicans. [!! *Interpret the meaning of the slope coefficient estimate of −3.38 for REPUBLICAN.*] Its partial slope coefficient estimate of −3.38 implies that the average number of groups lobbying a representative was 3.38 lower for a Republican than for a Democrat having the same scores on the remaining independent variables. [!! *Interpret the meaning of the slope coefficient estimate of 0.69 for CONTRIBUT-ING GROUPS.*] Finally, the partial slope coefficient estimate of 0.69 for **CONTRIBUTING GROUPS** suggests that, holding all other independent variables constant, an increase of one in the total number of groups supportive of a broad-based tax that made a campaign contribution to a member prompted an average increase of 0.69 in the total number of groups lobbying the member for a broad-based tax.

Note that the slope coefficient estimate having the smallest numerical value—that for **IDEOLOGY**—has the largest t-statistic. At first glance, this may seem perplexing. But one cannot interpret the meaning of an unstandardized partial slope coefficient—or gauge how strong an effect it reflects—without knowledge of the measurement scales for the independent and dependent variables. If Wright had divided his scores for **IDEOLOGY** by 100 before conducting the regression analysis, so that his measure ranged from 0 to 1 instead of 0 to 100, his coefficient estimate for **IDEOLOGY** would have been −10 (i.e., 100 times the estimate of −0.10 that he reported). The coefficient estimate would have been larger in numerical value, but it would have reflected an effect of the same magnitude as the published estimate of −0.10. The lesson here is clear. You should be careful to avoid the trap of viewing a partial slope coefficient of, say, 0.00000056 as obviously indicating a weak impact, but one of 560,000 as implying a strong impact, just because 0.00000056 is a "small" number and 560,000 is "large." Depending on the measurement scales for variables, 0.00000056 might indicate a strong effect and 560,000 a weak one.

Population Dynamics and Economic Development

In an article in the *American Sociological Review,* Edward M. Crenshaw, Ansari Z. Ameen, and Matthew Christenson (1997) use multiple regression analysis to clarify the relationship between population growth and economic growth in fifty-four developing countries. They note that previous research on this topic generally concludes that higher population growth leads to lower economic growth, as "rapid population growth forces scarce capital to be spent on nonproductive segments of the population (e.g., children) and encourages undercapitalization of the economy, underemployment, low wages, and anemic market demand" (p. 974). However, the authors contend that the relationship between population growth and economic growth is more complicated than these arguments would suggest. They claim that "the influence of population growth on economic growth depends on the *age* structure of the population" so that an increase in the child population may indeed slow economic growth, but a growing labor force should increase economic growth (p. 976). (You may refer to the original article for a thorough presentation of prior work in this area and more details about the authors' theoretical arguments.)

To test this claim, Crenshaw et al. employ the following regression model:

$$
\begin{aligned}
(5.2) \quad \text{GDP GROWTH}_i = {} & b_0 + b_1 \text{PER CAPITA GDP}_i + \\
& b_2 \text{POPULATION GROWTH UNDER 15}_i + \\
& b_3 \text{POPULATION GROWTH OVER 15}_i + \\
& b_4 \text{CHANGE IN GROSS DOMESTIC INVESTMENT}_i + \\
& b_5 \text{CHANGE IN FOREIGN INVESTMENT}_i + e_i
\end{aligned}
$$

The dependent variable, **GDP GROWTH**$_i$, equals the average annual percentage change in real per capita gross domestic product (GDP) in country *i* over the period of 1965 to 1990. Two independent variables enable Crenshaw et al. to measure the effects of population growth on economic growth. **POPULATION GROWTH UNDER 15**$_i$ measures the average annual percentage change in the population below age 15 in country *i* over the period of 1965 to 1980, and **POPULATION GROWTH OVER 15**$_i$ measures the same value in the population *above* age 15. On the basis of the theoretical arguments presented in the previous paragraph, the authors expect b_2 to be negative and b_3 to be positive. The variable **PER CAPITA GDP**$_i$, which measures per capita GDP in 1965, is included because the authors argue that nations with higher initial levels of per capita GDP are likely to have lower rates of economic growth. Therefore, they expect that b_1 will be negative. The model also includes two additional economic variables: **CHANGE IN GROSS DOMESTIC INVESTMENT**$_i$, which denotes the average annual percentage change in gross domestic investment over the period of 1970 to 1980 in country *i*, and **CHANGE IN FOREIGN INVESTMENT**$_i$, which indicates the average annual percentage change in direct private foreign investment over the period of 1967 to 1978. Because both of these factors reflect economic benefits, the authors expect b_4 and b_5 to be positive.

There are several important elements of research design embodied in equation 5.2. First, like most social science research, the model postulated by Crenshaw et al. involves a specific statement of causation: that a nation's population change affects its economic growth. Recall, however, that regression analysis—or any other nonexperimental research—cannot provide definitive evidence of causation. The authors of this study recognize at least one alternative theory of causation to the one they propose: that "economic change may affect fertility and mortality" and thus population change (p. 977). Because of these two conflicting theories, observing a relationship between population change and economic growth will not necessarily settle the question about which of these variables causes the other. Crenshaw et al. are sensitive to this possibility and confront it by calculating economic growth over the period of 1965 to 1990 but calculating the population growth variables only through 1980. This, the authors argue (p. 977), is sufficient to establish that any relationship between population change and economic growth cannot be due to an effect of the latter on the former. It is a simple matter of logic that if a change in X occurs *before* a change in Y, then the change in Y cannot possibly be the cause of the change in X. (Of course, when evaluating this article, it is appropriate for you to form your own conclusion about the authors' theoretical arguments.)

Notice that the model used by Crenshaw et al. contains five independent variables, though only two (**POPULATION GROWTH UNDER 15** and **POPULATION GROWTH OVER 15**) are directly relevant to the authors' theoretical question. The remaining variables serve as statistical controls, allowing the authors to measure the effects of population growth on economic growth while holding the other variables constant. If their regression model excluded significant causes of economic growth that were correlated with population growth, the assumption that the disturbance term is uncorrelated with each independent variable would likely be violated, and we could not be confident that the estimated coefficients accurately reflect the effects of population growth. (When evaluating this or any other research, you should think carefully about other possible causes of the dependent variable that might have been excluded, potentially resulting in a violation of assumption 5.)

How well does this model satisfy the other assumptions of multiple regression? All independent variables in the model are measured at the interval level, which satisfies assumption 1. Since the dependent variable is measured as a percentage, it is continuous, which satisfies assumption 2. Assumption 3, namely, that all variables have been measured without error, probably has not been satisfied. The variables used here, representing various demographic and economic characteristics of a nation, certainly have not been measured *perfectly,* as no endeavor of data collection could accurately count every single individual or properly value every economic transaction in a nation. (Indeed, the amount of measurement error may vary across nations, since highly developed countries can be expected to have better data collection capabilities than less developed nations.) Moreover, governments may purposely inflate reported values of indicators of economic growth and activity to make their regimes look more successful. Another problem arises from the different measurement periods of some of the independent variables. The authors note that these choices are constrained by the availability of data, but they offer no explicit reason why **CHANGE IN FOREIGN INVESTMENT** should be measured from 1967 to 1978 and **CHANGE IN GROSS DOMESTIC INVESTMENT** from 1970 to 1980.

Does the model postulated by Crenshaw et al. satisfy assumptions 4 and 6, namely, that the effects of all independent variables are linear and additive? Crenshaw et al. suggest no reason to believe otherwise. However, as with our previous example, readers should consider each independent variable and ask themselves whether the effect of that variable might be expected to vary with the value of that or any other independent variable in the model. If there are any answers in the affirmative, then one or both of these regression assumptions would be violated.

TABLE 5.2   Crenshaw, Ameen, and Christenson's Model of GDP Growth

	Population Coefficient	Coefficient Estimate	t-statistic
Intercept	b_0	2.08*	1.95
PER CAPITA GDP	b_1	−1.05**	−2.88
POPULATION GROWTH UNDER 15	b_2	−1.81**	−4.63
POPULATION GROWTH OVER 15	b_3	1.57**	3.84
CHANGE IN GROSS DOMESTIC INVESTMENT	b_4	0.10*	2.37
CHANGE IN FOREIGN INVESTMENT	b_5	0.06**	3.25

$R^2 = 0.76$.
* Statistically significant at .05 level.
** Statistically significant at .01 level.

SOURCE: Table 2 from Crenshaw, Ameen, and Christenson 1997.

Crenshaw et al. believe that one of the assumptions about the error term that we have avoided discussing in detail has not been satisfied in their model. Specifically, they find evidence of heteroscedasticity. To address this problem, they use a statistical procedure called *White's correction*. Until you have studied statistics and taken advanced courses on regression analysis, you can only accept the authors' assertion that this procedure is necessary. Fortunately, however, White's correction has no effect whatsoever on the interpretations of the coefficient estimates of the model.

Using cross-sectional data for the fifty-four countries in their sample, Crenshaw et al. obtained the OLS coefficient estimates listed in Table 5.2. The model's R^2 value is 0.76. [!! *Interpret the meaning of the R^2 value of 0.76.*] This can be interpreted to mean that the independent variables collectively explain 76 percent of the variation in nations' economic growth.

The regression results demonstrate that the coefficients for the three variables included as statistical controls are statistically significant in the predicted direction. Yet for one of the variables, the lack of clarity of the measurement unit makes it impossible to determine the substantive significance of the estimated effect. The authors indicate that **PER CAPITA GDP** is measured in thousands of "1985 international dollars," but they fail to define this measurement unit. Since we do not know what one unit is, we cannot interpret what the slope coefficient estimate of −1.05 means. Fortunately, the measurement units for the other variables are identified, permitting more meaningful interpretations. For example, the coefficient estimate for **CHANGE IN GROSS DO-MESTIC INVESTMENT** is 0.10. [!! *Interpret the meaning of the slope coefficient estimate of 0.10 for CHANGE IN GROSS DOMES-TIC INVESTMENT.*] This implies that a one-point increase in a nation's average annual percentage change in gross domestic investment (over the period of 1970–1980) increases the country's expected annual percentage change in GDP (over the period of 1965–1990) by about one-tenth of one percentage point when all other independent variables are held constant.

Turning to the variables of primary theoretical interest, we see that the results presented in Table 5.2 provide support for the authors' hypotheses about the effect of population growth on economic growth. The coefficient estimate for **POPULATION GROWTH OVER 15** is 1.57, and that for **POPULATION GROWTH UNDER 15** is −1.81 (both of which are statistically significant at the .01 level). [!! *Interpret the meaning of each of these slope coefficient estimates.*] Thus, holding all other independent variables constant, an increase of one point in the average annual percentage change in population *over* age 15 *increases* the expected annual percentage change in GDP by 1.57 points, whereas an increase of one point in the average annual percentage change in population *under* 15 *decreases* the expected annual percentage change in GDP by 1.81 points.

6

Advanced Topics

In this chapter we present several topics that go beyond the basics of regression analysis. Whereas the material covered so far is likely to be of use for understanding virtually any application of regression, the extensions of the core regression model covered in this chapter are more advanced and have more limited applicability. It is probably unrealistic to expect yourself to master the individual topics in this part of the book to the same degree that you master the material on basic regression. Thus, we recommend that you read through the sections that follow to gain some familiarity with the topics covered, and then treat them as reference material. For example, if you find yourself faced with an article that uses probit analysis, you can review the section on that topic in this chapter to refresh your memory before reading the study.

Interaction vs. Nonlinearity

The regression assumptions that the effects of independent variables are linear (assumption 4) and additive (assumption 6) are easy to confuse. This is because both assumptions require that the effect of each independent variable remains constant when the values of one or more variables change. But effects can fail to be constant in two different ways. We call the effect of an independent variable *nonlinear* when its impact on the dependent variable varies with the value of that independent variable. In contrast, we say that a variable's effect is *interactive* when its impact on the dependent variable shifts with the value of *other* independent variables. The following two sections describe how social scientists modify the basic regression model to allow for interactive and nonlinear effects.

Interactive Models

Suppose we hypothesize that four independent variables—X_1, X_2, X_3, and X_4—influence a dependent variable, Y. Furthermore, we believe that the effects of X_1 and X_2 are constant; the impact of each is the same regardless of the values of the four independent variables. However, we believe that X_3 and X_4 interact in influencing Y such that the effect of X_3 on Y varies with the value of X_4. These hypotheses can be incorporated in a regression model by using a *multiplicative* (or *product*) term involving X_3 and X_4:

$$(6.1) \quad Y_i = b_0 + b_1X_{1i} + b_2X_{2i} + b_3X_{3i} + b_4X_{4i} + b_5M_i + e_i,$$

where $M_i = X_{3i} \times X_{4i}$; that is, for each case, M is a variable constructed by multiplying together the values of X_3 and X_4 for the case. Why does including the multiplicative term $X_3 \times X_4$ specify interaction between X_3 and X_4?

The inclusion of $X_3 \times X_4$ makes it so that the effect of X_3 on Y varies with the value of X_4. We can confirm this with a bit of algebra, and it will be easiest to follow the math if we use an illustration involving specific numbers for the coefficients (b_0, b_1, b_2, b_3, b_4, and b_5). Assume that X_4 can vary between 0 and 10 in the population of interest, and that the coefficients for equation 6.1 are as follows:

$$(6.2) \ Y_i = 5 + (8)X_{1i} - (6)X_{2i} + (4)X_{3i} + (2)X_{4i} + (3)(X_{3i} \times X_{4i}) + e_i,$$

where we have rewritten M as the product of its components. We can compare the effect of X_3 on Y across three different values of X_4: the lowest possible value (0), the highest value (10), and some midrange value (e.g., 5). First, we see how equation 6.2 simplifies when we fix X_4 at zero; we "plug in" zero for X_4 and obtain

$$Y_i = 5 + (8)X_{1i} - (6)X_{2i} + (4)X_{3i} + (2)(0) + (3)(X_{3i})(0) + e_i.$$

Canceling products that equal zero gives

$$(6.3) Y_i = 5 + (8)X_{1i} - (6)X_{2i} + (4)X_{3i} + e_i \text{ [with } X_4 \text{ fixed at zero]}.$$

Note that X_4 has been eliminated and equation 6.3 takes the form of a "regular" (additive) regression model with three independent variables—X_1, X_2, and X_3. (In other words, since we have fixed X_4 at the specific value of zero, X_4 is no longer a variable.) The partial slope coefficient of 4 for X_3 in equation 6.3 implies that *when X_4 is zero*, and when X_1 and X_2 are held constant at any values, a one-unit increase in X_3 results in an increase of four in the expected value of Y.

Next, we fix X_4 in equation 6.2 at the midrange value, 5, and get

$$Y_i = 5 + (8)X_{1i} - (6)X_{2i} + (4)X_{3i} + (2)(5) + (3)(X_{3i})(5) + e_i.$$

Combining terms yields

$$Y_i = [5 + (2)(5)] + (8)X_{1i} - (6)X_{2i} + (4 + 15)X_{3i} + e_i,$$

and after doing some arithmetic we obtain

$$Y_i = 15 + (8)X_{1i} - (6)X_{2i} + (19)X_{3i} + e_i \text{ [with } X_4 \text{ fixed at 5]}.$$

[!! *Try to interpret the meaning of the slope coefficient of 19 for X_3.*] The slope coefficient of 19 for X_3 in this equation means that *when X_4 is fixed at 5*, and X_1 and X_2 are fixed at any values, a one-unit increase in X_3 prompts an increase of 19 in the expected value of Y.

Finally, a similar calculation shows that when X_4 takes on its maximum value of 10, equation 6.2 simplifies to

$$Y_i = 25 + (8)X_{1i} - (6)X_{2i} + (34)X_{3i} + e_i \text{ [with } X_4 \text{ fixed at 10]}.$$

[!! *Interpret the meaning of the slope coefficient of 34 for X_3.*] This means that *when X_4 is held constant at its maximum value of 10*, a one-unit increase in X_3 leads to a 34-unit increase in the expected value of Y. Thus, we see that as X_4 increases from its minimum value (0) to its maximum value (10), the slope coefficient expressing the impact of X_3 on Y increases from 4 to 34. The substantive meaning of this result depends on the interpretations attached to slopes of 4 and 34; if 4 reflects a weak effect and 34 a strong effect, then the interaction between X_3 and X_4 is strong. If instead 34 reflects a weak effect and 4 a *very* weak effect, one would describe the interaction as weak. In any event, through the procedure of fixing one of the variables in a product term at a variety of values, we have succeeded in calculating slopes that describe the changing nature of the impact of the other independent variable. This basic procedure works in any interactive regression model with a multiplicative term.

As an example of an interactive regression model, consider a study by Khalid A. Al-Sharideh and W. Richard Goe (1998) in the journal *Research in Higher Education*. Al-Sharideh and Goe seek to explain the effect of cultural assimilation and friendships (among other variables) on the level of self-esteem among foreign students at American institutions of higher education. They administered a survey to a sample of 226 foreign students from among those enrolled at Kansas State University, measuring (among other variables) **SELF-ESTEEM**, defined with a set of questions relating to individual self-esteem; **ASSIMILATION**, based on a set of questions concerning individual knowledge of and favorability toward American culture; and **COCULTURALS**, equal to the number of local friends from a culture similar to that of the respondent. In their theoretical argument, the authors state that "the formation of strong ties with other people of a similar cultural background (i.e., participation in an ethnic community) by an international student serves to condition the influence of assimilating American culture . . . on the personal adjustment of the student. Specifically, once an international student establishes a network of strong ties with other people with a common cultural background . . . the assimilation of American culture . . . [becomes] unimportant in influencing the student's personal adjustment" (p. 705). In other words, **ASSIMILATION** has little or no effect on **SELF-ESTEEM** when **COCULTURALS** takes on a high value. Thus, Al-Sharideh and Goe hypothesize interaction: the effect of **ASSIMILATION** on **SELF-ESTEEM** varies with the value of **COCULTURALS**.

To test this hypothesis, Al-Sharideh and Goe estimate the coefficients for a regression model with **SELF-ESTEEM** as the dependent

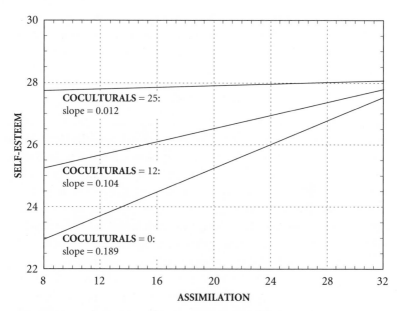

FIGURE 6.1   Al-Sharideh and Goe's interactive model
SOURCE: Constructed from information in Al-Sharideh and Goe 1998.

variable and **ASSIMILATION, COCULTURALS,** and the multiplicative term **ASSIMILATION × COCULTURALS** among the independent variables. Given the coefficient estimates, we can fix one of the independent variables (**COCULTURALS**) in the product term at several different values and compute the effect of the other independent variable (**ASSIMILATION**) at these values (fixing all other independent variables at their average values in the sample). When **COCULTURALS** is zero (i.e., when a respondent has no friends of a similar culture), the slope of the effect of **ASSIMILATION** on **SELF-ESTEEM** equals 0.189. This effect is depicted by the lowest of the lines in Figure 6.1. When **COCULTURALS** is equal to 12—which is the average value in the sample—the effect of **ASSIMILATION** is characterized by the middle line in the graph, which has a slope of 0.104. Finally, when **COCULTURALS** is fixed at 25, among the highest number of ties with friends sharing the same culture in the sample, the slope estimate for **ASSIMILATION** is only 0.012.   The slopes of the three lines in Figure 6.1 demonstrate that, as expected, the effect of the assimilation of foreign students on their level of self-esteem declines as their contact with friends sharing their native culture increases.

Nonlinear Models

As we have seen, the basic multivariate regression model assumes that all independent variables are linearly related to the dependent variable, that is, that the effect of each independent variable on the dependent variable is the same regardless of the value of that independent variable. However, in some contexts, *linear* regression models may not accurately reflect the hypotheses being tested. For example, consider the effect of age on participation in politics (via voting, contacting legislators, campaign contributions, etc.). We might expect age to be positively related to participation, since young adults tend not to be very interested in politics, and with increasing age comes greater interest. However, at some age, declining physical ability to participate may become a factor, so that the relationship between age and participation weakens or even becomes negative. For this reason, many political scientists have modeled the effect of age on political participation as a nonlinear one.

One common way of modeling nonlinear effects is with a *polynomial* equation. A polynomial equation is an equation that includes one or more *powers* of an independent variable X (i.e., X^2, X^3, etc.). It turns out that a polynomial equation yields a curve that slopes positively in some ranges and negatively in others. If we refer to a location in which the slope shifts from positive to negative (or vice versa) as a "bend" in the curve, the number of "bends" is one less than the highest power of X included in the model.

For instance, we might specify that the effect of X on Y varies according to the value of X in the following regression equation:

$$(6.4) \qquad Y = b_0 + b_1 X_i + b_2 X_i^2 + e_i.$$

This type of polynomial, in which the highest power of X is X^2, is called a *quadratic* equation, and the curve it describes has a

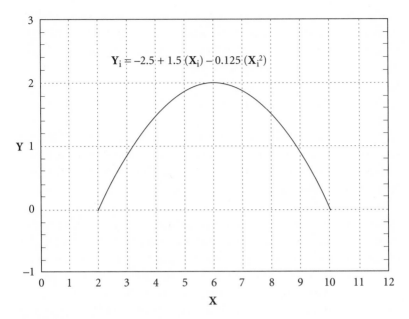

$$Y_i = -2.5 + 1.5 (X_i) - 0.125 (X_i^2)$$

FIGURE 6.2   A quadratic equation

single bend in it. Figure 6.2 presents an example of a quadratic equation.

A quadratic equation can be used to capture a wide variety of nonlinear relationships. The most obvious use of an equation like that in Figure 6.2 is when an independent variable, X, has a positive effect on Y (of declining strength) when X is below a certain value (in Figure 6.2, when X is less than 6), but a negative effect on Y (of increasing magnitude) when X is above that value. However, if the measurement scale for X allows only values less than 6, then the equation graphed in Figure 6.2 can be used to reflect an independent variable that always has a positive effect on Y, but one of decreasing magnitude as X increases. Also, changing the signs of the coefficients for X and X^2 (from positive to negative, and vice versa) turns the curve upside down so that the single bend occurs at the bottom. Thus, a quadratic model is quite flexible in terms of the kinds of nonlinear relationships it can reflect.

You should also know that it is possible for polynomial regression models to involve a mixture of linear and nonlinear effects;

some variables can be specified to have nonlinear relationships with the dependent variable (with powers of these variables included in the equation), and others can be assumed to have linear effects. For example, in the equation

$$Y = b_0 + b_1 X_{1i} + b_2 X_{2i} + b_3 X_{3i} + b_4 X_{3i}^2 + b_5 X_{4i} + b_6 X_{4i}^2 + e_i,$$

X_1's and X_2's effects are assumed to be linear, and those of X_3 and X_4 are presumed nonlinear. Finally, you should be aware that a polynomial equation is only one of a number of nonlinear equations that analysts may use.

Whether a nonlinear equation is quadratic, or is another type of polynomial, or takes some other form, the interpretation of coefficients for nonlinear models is not as straightforward as that for linear models. In a nonlinear model we can no longer interpret the partial slope coefficient for X as the change in the expected value of Y arising from a one-unit increase in X. This is because it no longer makes sense to talk about the change in Y resulting from an increase of one unit in X *without specifying the starting value of X.* Indeed, the whole point of a nonlinear model is that the effect of X on Y varies with the value of X. This can be seen clearly in Figure 6.2. When X increases from 2 to 3, Y increases by 0.875 units (from 0 to 0.875); when X increases from 3 to 4, Y increases by 0.625 units (from 0.875 to 1.50); and when X increases from 4 to 5, Y increases by only 0.375 units (from 1.50 to 1.875). Well-written articles relying on a polynomial model—or any other nonlinear equation—clarify for readers the effects of an independent variable X by describing how the estimated slope of the relationship between X and Y varies over the range of X. This information on varying slopes can appear in a graph like that shown in Figure 6.2, in a table, or in the text of the study.

For example, consider an article by S. P. Raj (1995) in the *Journal of Marketing.* Raj uses a nonlinear equation to model consumer purchasing habits in eighty-six product categories (including canned soup, canned cat food, toothpaste, aluminum foil, and cigarettes). He hypothesizes that the total number of brands available in a product category (denoted **BRANDS**) will have a nonlinear effect on consumer loyalty within that category (denoted **LOYALTY** and

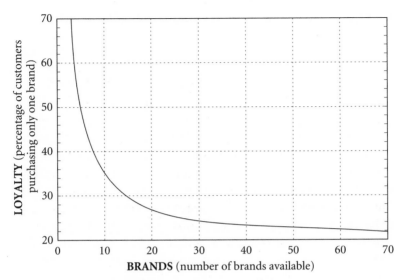

FIGURE 6.3   Raj's nonlinear model
SOURCE: Raj 1995.

measured as the percentage of consumers who purchase only one brand in the product category). Specifically, he believes that the number of brands should always have a negative relationship with consumer loyalty but that the relationship should decline in magnitude as the number of brands increases. After specifying a nonlinear model, Raj presents a graph of the estimated relationship between the number of brands and product loyalty (reproduced in Figure 6.3). The graph shows that as the number of brands of a product increases from three (the sample minimum) to nine, the loyalty measure declines from about 70 percent to about 35 percent, but that when the number of brands is greater than nine, the rate of decline in loyalty is much slower, so that when there are seventy brands of a product, the loyalty variable has declined to only about 22 percent. Raj summarizes this finding by stating that "as number of brands increases, loyalty levels decline sharply at first and then begin to level off" (p. 58). Thus, by applying a nonlinear specification to consumer data, Raj is able to demonstrate not only that there is a negative relationship between the number of brands in a product category and consumer loyalty within that category but also that the strength of this relationship changes according to the number of brands available.

Dichotomous Dependent Variables: Probit and Logit

Recall that one of the assumptions of regression analysis is that the dependent variable is continuous. However, there are many research questions for which the dependent variable violates this assumption. For example, one might be interested in the factors influencing whether an individual will get married, or the impact of an independent variable on whether a firm will adopt a specific innovative management tool in a particular year. In both cases, the dependent variable is dichotomous and can be conceived as whether a particular event (e.g., a marriage or an adoption of an innovation) occurs. Most social scientists analyzing a dichotomous dependent variable Y assign the variable a score of 1 if the event occurs and 0 if it does not. They then frame their hypotheses in terms of the effects of independent variables on the probability that Y = 1. For example, for a study of the marriage behavior of single women, we could code the event of a marriage during a given year as 1 and the absence of a marriage as 0, and propose the hypothesis that women who are employed have a smaller probability of getting married (i.e., a smaller probability that Y = 1) than women who do not hold jobs.

One tempting possibility for estimating the coefficients of a model with a dichotomous dependent variable is to ignore the fact that the dependent variable is not continuous, and use OLS regression analysis. There are a variety of statistical reasons why this is inappropriate, and you will learn about them in future methods course work. But perhaps the most important reason to eschew the use of regression analysis with dichotomous dependent variables is substantive in nature. In models with dichotomous dependent variables, it is likely that the assumption that independent variables have linear effects does not hold.

For example, consider a model seeking to analyze the factors that determine whether a family owns a home. The dependent variable, which we might label **HOME**, would be coded 0 for families that do not own homes and 1 for families that do. One reasonable hypothesis is that a family's income has a positive effect on the probability that it owns a home (that is, the probability that **HOME** = 1). It would be unreasonable, however, to expect this impact to be the same at all levels of income. At moderate income levels, the effect might be quite strong. For a family with an annual income of $40,000, a change of $5,000 could substantially influence whether it could afford a home, and thus the family's probability of home ownership. Yet, at the extremes of the income scale—say, for families whose income is less than $20,000 or greater than $200,000—we would not expect an income change of $5,000 to affect the probability of home ownership a great deal. Rather, low-income families should be very unlikely to own a home, and high-income families should be quite likely to own a home, and incremental changes in income are unlikely to affect these probabilities very much. If our reasoning is correct, then family income would have a nonlinear effect on the probability of home ownership, and therefore OLS regression analysis would be inappropriate.

Similar stories of nonlinearity can be told about most other variables that have effects on dichotomous dependent variables. Fortunately, statisticians have developed alternatives to OLS regression that are suitable for models with dichotomous dependent variables. You will learn more about these techniques, called *logit* or *probit*, in future methods courses. For now, though, you should be pleased to know that these techniques are similar to regression in many ways. We can still estimate coefficients that allow us to assess the effects of the independent variables on the dependent variable, and we can determine whether these coefficients are statistically significant. However, logit and probit models depart from OLS regression in an important respect. Although logit and probit analysis yield a coefficient estimate for each independent variable, one cannot arrive at a simple interpretation of the impact of an independent variable on the basis of a quick inspection of the coefficient for that variable. Determining the effect of an independent variable requires more extensive analysis.

As an example of research with a dichotomous dependent variable, consider a paper by David R. Johnson and Laurie K. Scheuble (1995), which appeared in the *Journal of Marriage and the Family*. The authors seek to explain "whether or not a woman will make a nonconventional marital name choice." The dependent variable, **MARITAL NAME CHOICE**, is set at 0 if a woman makes a "conventional" choice to take her husband's last name as her own and drop her original last name completely, and is set at 1 if she makes any other choice—defined as "keeping her birth name as a middle or last name, hyphenating, or other nonconventional choices" (p. 726). Johnson and Scheuble speculate that a woman's age at marriage has a positive effect on the probability that she will make a nonconventional name choice (i.e., the probability that **MARITAL NAME CHOICE** = 1) because "women who married at a later age . . . had more time to establish an adult identity with their birth name" (p. 725). To test this hypothesis, the authors use *logistic regression* (another name for logit) to estimate a model having marital name choice as the dependent variable and age at marriage among the independent variables.

The authors find that, as hypothesized, age at marriage has a positive and statistically significant coefficient estimate. As discussed earlier, the value of this coefficient is not sufficient to identify the effect of marriage age on the probability of an unconventional name choice. It is possible, however, to use the logit coefficients for the model to calculate the predicted probability that a woman with any specified set of values for the independent variables in the model will make an unconventional name choice. It turns out that in any logit (or probit) model, the effect of an independent variable X on the probability that Y = 1 depends not only on the value of X but also on the values of all other independent variables. In Figure 6.4 we show the estimated relationship between marriage age and the probability of an unconventional name choice when each of the other independent variables is fixed at a typical value in the sample. The graph confirms that marriage age is positively related to the probability of a nonconventional name choice. But note that this relationship is not linear; the estimated effect becomes stronger as marriage age increases. For example, when marriage age increases (by four years) from 20 to 24, the probability of a nonconventional choice increases by about 0.015, but when marriage age increases (again by four years) from 40 to 44, the probability of an unconventional choice increases by about 0.030—twice as large an increase.

We should point out that Johnson and Scheuble do not report the information contained in Figure 6.4 in their article; rather, we

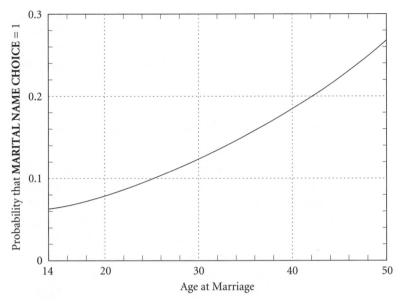

FIGURE 6.4   Estimated effects in Johnson and Scheuble's logit model
SOURCE: Constructed from information in Johnson and Scheuble 1995.

calculated these probabilities using the coefficients and the sample information provided by the authors. Indeed, even though the authors' hypotheses concern the effects of variables on the probability of a nonconventional name choice, they do not report any interpretations of their results in terms of the effects of variables on this probability. This detracts from the value of the research. Unfortunately, this shortcoming is not uncommon in studies relying on probit or logit; often, authors do not calculate estimates of the effects of the independent variables on the probability that $Y = 1$. Sometimes authors pay attention solely to the sign (positive or negative) and the level of statistical significance of the estimated coefficients, which, as we have seen, does not provide any information about the substantive strength of the effects of the independent variables.[1] Unfortunately, until you have more advanced

---

[1]Authors also may provide information about "odds ratios" (this is only with logit, and not probit), which represent the ratio of the probability that $Y = 1$ to the probability that $Y = 0$.

training in statistical methods, if an author fails to provide you with estimates of the effects of variables on the probability that $Y = 1$, you may have to be satisfied with learning only whether these effects are positive or negative and whether they are statistically significant.

Multi-equation Models: Simultaneous Equation Models and Recursive Causal Models

Multivariate regression equations assess the effect of each independent variable on a single dependent variable. However, in some circumstances researchers wish to go beyond the confines of a single equation. One reason to do so might be that they expect causal effects between a pair of variables to run "in both directions." In that case, instead of a hypothesis that an independent variable affects a dependent variable, the hypothesis is that two variables (Y_1 and Y_2) influence each other: Y_1 affects Y_2, and Y_2 affects Y_1. This hypothesis is meant to suggest that a change in the value of Y_1 should prompt a change in the value of Y_2, and that this change in turn leads Y_1 to change. For example, individuals who spend more time watching the news on television should become more interested in public affairs, but at the same time, individuals who are more interested in public affairs should pay greater attention to news outlets.

When researchers hypothesize that Y_1 and Y_2 influence each other, they specify a multi-equation model. One equation has Y_2 as the dependent variable and Y_1 as one of the independent variables; a second equation reverses this, making Y_1 the dependent variable and Y_2 an independent variable. Such multi-equation models are called *simultaneous equation models* or *nonrecursive models*. The most common technique for estimating the coefficients of a simultaneous equation model is *two-stage least squares* (it is also referred to as the *instrumental variables* technique), and you will learn more about its origins and its properties in your future training in methodology. (Another technique researchers use is *three-stage least squares*.) For now, you should note that with simultaneous equation models, one interprets the coefficients one equation at a time. Furthermore, for each equation, each variable's coefficient can be interpreted just as though it were a partial slope coefficient in a single-equation regression model.

In other circumstances, researchers are interested not only in the effects of each of several independent variables on the dependent variable but also in the effects of some of the independent variables on *other* independent variables. In this situation, researchers specify another type of multi-equation model, referred to as a *recursive causal model* or *path analysis*. For example, if X_1 and X_2 both affect Y, and in addition X_1 influences X_2, one equation would have Y as the dependent variable and include X_1 and X_2 as independent variables, and a second equation would make X_2 the dependent variable and have X_1 as the independent variable:

(6.5) $$Y_i = b_0 + b_1 X_{1i} + b_2 X_{2i} + e_i.$$

(6.6) $$X_{2i} = c_0 + c_1 X_{1i} + e_i.$$

(We use the letter "c" for coefficients in equation 6.6 instead of "b" to differentiate them from the coefficients in equation 6.5.) Note that if X_1 and X_2 both affect Y, and in addition X_1 affects X_2, then there are two kinds of effects of X_1 on Y: the *direct* effect of X_1 on Y, and the so-called *indirect* effect. The indirect effect refers to any changes that X_1 prompts in Y by virtue of its causing a change in X_2, which in turn (due to X_2's effect on Y) leads to a change in Y.

Researchers estimate the effects in a recursive causal model— like that of equations 6.5 and 6.6—by using OLS regression on each equation separately. The coefficient estimates for these equations can be interpreted just as though they were partial slope coefficients in a single-equation model, and the effects these coefficients reflect are those we call *direct* effects. Thus, the slope coefficient b_2 reflects the direct effect of X_2 on Y. Also, b_1 captures the direct effect of X_1 on Y, and c_1 describes the direct effect of X_1 on X_2. To figure out the *indirect* effect of X_1 on Y in this model, we must take into account both the direct effect of X_1 on X_2 (i.e., c_1) and the direct effect of X_2 on Y (i.e., b_2). (It turns out that when standardized coefficients are used—see Chapter 4—the indirect effect is calculated as the product of c_1 and b_2, a point that may or may not seem intuitively clear; if not, do not be concerned.)

As an example, let us consider a study by Shirley Taylor (1994) published in the *Journal of Marketing.* Taylor uses path analysis to study the determinants of service evaluations among a sample of airline passengers whose flights had been delayed. As part of her recursive causal model, Taylor considers the relationships among three variables: FILLED TIME, defined as the passenger's report of how completely their time was filled during the delay; UNCERTAINTY, defined as the extent to which the passenger felt uncertain, anxious, uneasy, and unsettled as a result of the delay; and ANGER, defined as the extent to which the passenger felt irritated, annoyed, angry, and frustrated about the delay. Taylor argues that FILLED TIME affects ANGER and UNCERTAINTY, because airline passengers who are exposed to stimuli (such as interaction with associates or fellow passengers, or reading) during a delay "pay less attention to the delay itself, resulting in less attention being paid to factors creating uncertainty and anger." In addition, Taylor notes that uncertainty "makes planning around the delay impossible for the customer" and "doesn't allow the customer the power to deal with the delay," thus increasing the customer's feelings of anger (i.e., UNCERTAINTY affects ANGER) (p. 59). Hence when Taylor considers the effect of FILLED TIME on ANGER, she hypothesizes two types of impacts: a direct effect of FILLED TIME on ANGER, and an indirect effect, whereby FILLED TIME affects UNCERTAINTY, which in turn affects ANGER. (Taylor's model also includes the direct and indirect effects of several other variables; we refer the interested reader to the original article for more details.) The results demonstrate that FILLED TIME does indeed have a direct negative effect on ANGER as well as an indirect negative effect operating through UNCERTAINTY, with the direct effect about 50 percent larger than the indirect effect. (This comparison of the magnitudes of direct and indirect effects is only possible if *standardized* coefficients have been estimated.)

7

Conclusion

This book was written especially for new students of social science. Presumably such students gradually achieve greater levels of sophistication in their understanding of regression analysis and other forms of multivariate analysis as their training in statistics and research methods progresses. But we hope this volume helps students to realize that even before they study statistics, they can learn enough about multivariate analysis to understand at a basic level—and even to critically evaluate—empirical research relying on regression or other multivariate techniques. The most important requirement for such research is that it be based on *sound theory*. Recall that our insistence on a convincing theory would be our only protection against mistakenly concluding from bivariate regression analysis that fire trucks cause fire damage. Because a researcher's theoretical justification should be completely independent of the empirical analysis that tests the theory, students can evaluate the most critical aspect of research that relies on multivariate techniques even if they have no familiarity at all with either statistics or multivariate analysis.

The second most important requirement for good multivariate analysis is that the model accurately specify the theory being tested, that is, it should include all independent variables central to the theory and reflect any forms of interaction and nonlinearity hypothesized. If independent variables with strong effects on the dependent variable are excluded, it is likely, as we have seen, that the assumption that the error term is uncorrelated with each of the independent variables has been violated. Armed with only the information in this book, a student can go a good distance toward identifying when regression (or probit or logit) equations have been inaccurately specified. Finally, even students who have no training in statistics should be capable of detecting measurement error in a multivariate model by considering whether the measures chosen for variables actually reflect what the author intends to measure. If a reader of an article that presents statistical results assesses the soundness of the author's theory, whether the theory is accurately specified by the regression (or probit or logit) equation, and whether the variables in the equation have been measured well, the reader—even with no background in statistics—is quite likely to arrive at a reasonable assessment of the quality of the research reported.

Glossary

Additive effects   Two independent variables have additive effects on Y if the effect of each variable is the same regardless of the value of the other independent variable.

Categorical variable   A variable that takes on three or more values but is not measured at the interval level.

Continuous variable   An interval-level variable that is free to take on any numerical value.

Correlation coefficient   A measure of the strength of the relationship between two variables.

Dependent variable   In a causal hypothesis, the variable whose variation is explained.

Dichotomous variable   A variable that can take on only one of two possible values.

Error (or disturbance) term   The net effect of all variables influencing Y that are not included in a regression equation plus any inherent randomness in the process by which Y is determined. For a given case, the value of the error term is the amount by which the value of Y for the case deviates from the expected value of Y for a case having the same value for each independent variable as the case in question.

Independent variable   In a causal hypothesis, the variable that is expected to influence the dependent variable.

Interaction   Two variables interact in influencing Y if the effect of one variable on Y varies with the value of the other variable.

Intercept   In a regression model, the expected value of Y for a case for which the value of each of the independent variables is zero.

Interval-level measurement   Measurement in which any difference of one unit (e.g., the difference between scores of 6 and 7, or between scores of 53 and 54) reflects the same difference in the amount of the property being measured.

Multicollinearity   The presence of relationships among the independent variables in a regression model.

Ordinary least squares   A mathematical procedure that provides a unique best-fitting regression equation for a sample of cases.

Partial slope coefficient (in a multivariate regression model)   Interpreted as the change in the expected value of Y resulting from a one-unit increase in an independent variable when all other independent variables are held constant.

Polynomial equation   Equation that includes one or more powers of an independent variable X (i.e., X^2, X^3, etc.).

Population   The cases to which a hypothesis is meant to apply.

Quadratic equation   Polynomial equation in which the highest power of X is X^2.

R^2   A measure of the fit of a regression model, most commonly interpreted as the proportion of the variation in Y that is explained by the independent variables.

Slope coefficient in a bivariate regression model   Interpreted as the change in the expected value of Y resulting from a one-unit increase in X.

References

Al-Sharideh, Khalid A., and W. Richard Goe. 1998. "Ethnic Communities Within the University: An Examination of Factors Influencing the Personal Adjustment of International Students." *Research in Higher Education* 39:699–725.

Berry, William D. 1993. *Understanding Regression Assumptions.* Newbury Park, CA: Sage.

Crenshaw, Edward M., Ansari Z. Ameen, and Matthew Christenson. 1997. "Population Dynamics and Economic Development: Age-Specific Population Growth Rates and Economic Growth in Developing Countries, 1965 to 1990." *American Sociological Review* 62: 974–984.

Johnson, David R., and Laurie K. Scheuble. 1995. "Women's Marital Naming in Two Generations: A National Study." *Journal of Marriage and the Family* 57:724–732.

Kiser, Edgar, and Kriss A. Drass. 1987. "Changes in the Core of the World-System and the Production of Utopian Literature in Great Britain and the United States, 1883–1975." *American Sociological Review* 52:286–293.

Kone, Susan L., and Richard F. Winters. 1993. "Taxes and Voting: Electoral Retribution in the American States." *Journal of Politics* 55:22–40.

Maddala, G. S. 1992. *Introduction to Econometrics,* 2d ed. New York: Macmillan.

Raj, S. P. 1995. "Striking a Balance Between Brand 'Popularity' and Brand Loyalty." *Journal of Marketing* 49:53–59.

Ross, Catherine E., and Chia-ling Wu. 1995. "The Links Between Education and Health." *American Sociological Review* 60:719–745.

Taylor, Shirley. 1994. "Waiting for Service: The Relationship Between Delays and Evaluations of Service." *Journal of Marketing* 58:56–69.

Weisberg, Herbert F., Jon A. Krosnick, and Bruce D. Bowen. 1989. *An Introduction to Survey Research and Data Analysis.* 2d ed. Boston: Scott, Foresman and Company.

Wright, John R. 1990. "Contributions, Lobbying, and Committee Voting in the U.S. House of Representatives." *American Political Science Review* 84: 417–438.

Index